DELIGHTING

in

HIS PRESENCE

DELIGHTING
in
HIS PRESENCE

Daily Invitations
to Encounter Jesus
through Prayer and
Scripture

ERIC GILMOUR

DESTINY IMAGE® PUBLISHERS, INC.
P.O. Box 310, Shippensburg, PA 17257-0310
"Publishing cutting-edge prophetic resources to supernaturally empower the body of Christ"

This book and all other Destiny Image and Destiny Image Fiction books are available at Christian bookstores and distributors worldwide.

For more information on foreign distributors, call 717-532-3040.
Reach us on the Internet: www.destinyimage.com.

ISBN 13 TP: 978-0-7684-7836-5
ISBN 13 eBook: 978-0-7684-7837-2

For Worldwide Distribution, Printed in the U.S.A.
2 3 4 5 6 7 8 / 28 27 26 25 24

Contents

CHAPTER 1

A Calm Hour with God

For thus says the Lord God, the Holy One of Israel: "In returning and rest you shall be saved; in quietness and confidence shall be your strength…"

(Isaiah 30:15 NKJV).

When I first abandoned my life to the Lord in 1996, a man of God picked me up early in the morning for a road trip. As I sat there in the passenger seat, he turned to me and said, "Let's pray." I immediately started to rattle off in tongues, progressively getting louder with greater fervency and focus. I didn't know what else to do. I was mimicking what I had seen others do and thought that's what you do when you pray. Anyone looking at me would have thought I was in agony, making sounds, rocking back and forth in constant motion. This man of God waited patiently for me to finish machine-gunning God with tongues and desperate cries.

When the smoke finally cleared from my assault on God and war initiation with hell, the car became silent. Then with the steering wheel in one hand and his steaming coffee in the other, this man of God said softly, "Jesus, I worship You." He sat quietly and nearly whispered, "I worship You, precious Lamb of God. There is no one like You. I worship

You." In an instant, the undeniable presence of the Holy Spirit filled the car, deeply touching my heart.

The experience intrigued me. *How was he able to invoke God's presence with such ease?* I wondered. This man had not raised his voice or even appealed to God to manifest Himself. He had simply looked to Jesus in adoration. I learned an incredibly valuable lesson that day— *adoration is the secret to experiencing the conscious presence of God.* One ounce of adoration moves God more than any amount of effort and striving. This reminds me of something Canadian preacher and theologian, A. B. Simpson, is believed to have said when he saw people raising their voices in prayer, "People who are always yelling at God must live very far away from Him."

Dear reader, to gaze upon God in sweet fixation and loving worship is more valuable to God than any religious or human practice. Nothing is more humble than adoring Jesus. We must let this settle into our hearts as adoration puts us in our proper place and places Him in His as Lord over all.

Prayer must be understood to be the sustained fixation of the soul upon God. We must recognize that the blood that poured out from the flesh of the God-Man was to rend the veil over our eyes so that we could have an endless vision of Jesus. That is what prayer is— *"looking unto Jesus"* (Hebrews 12:1-2). This is the reconciliation: *the restoration of God and man in direct fellowship, finding pleasure in each other.* A. W. Tozer, the well-beloved author and American evangelical pastor, said it this way, "When the eyes of the soul looking out meet the eyes of God looking in, heaven has begun right here on this earth."[1]

True maturity in God is delighting in Him whether we ever receive the answers to our prayers. So many people have no idea that communion with God can be a great delight. As the Scottish preacher and writer Robert Murray McCheyne said, "A calm hour with God is worth a whole lifetime with man."[2] I submit to you that, not only can prayer be a great delight, but it should be the very source of all our delight. Dutch mystic John van Ruysbroeck wrote, "For while we please God and God pleases us, then love is practiced and eternal life."[3]

CHAPTER 2

Water and Life

My soul thirsts for You; my flesh longs for You in a dry and thirsty land where there is no water

(Psalm 63:1 NKJV).

Someone once asked me, "What is the world?" to which I felt inspired to answer, "The world is every feeble delight seeking to take the place of the Highest Delight, which is God Himself." Delight may be obtaining what we desire with our eyes. It may be the delight of obtaining the status we desire in our minds or obtaining the desires of our bodies. The entire world is set up to encourage these lower delights. But when such delights remain out of reach or are found to be unfulfilling, the result is dryness. Even things about God can take the place of God, and the result is the same. And the reason for this is because we have sought for something other than God to satiate our thirst.

His presence is our life. Many are weary in day-to-day living. They are tired and lack vitality. They are spiritually sluggish and slothful simply because, without the satisfaction that comes from enjoying God's presence and person, they have directed their pursuits amiss and, consequently, miss direct contact with God.

Too often, Christians have fashioned a concept of God's love based upon His incomparable action on their behalf alone. They along with us must understand that *His perfect sacrifice not only imparted a positional union with Him, but also the actual experience of union with Him.*[4] God's great love, revealed in the splendid spectacle upon Calvary, is experienced through the presence of the Spirit. It's the Spirit who pours out God's love into our hearts (see Romans 5:5). This image of pouring has truths of experience within it. The Spirit, the One who pours, contacts our vessels as the liquid love enters and fills us. An empty vessel is to be filled, and a filled vessel carries the substance.

Our souls' loving devotion is perpetuated by the enjoyment of the love of God. In Psalm 63:4 (NKJV), David says, *"Thus I will bless You while I live."* The whole of the writer's life was dedicated to the honor and admiration of Him who is sought by the soul, the Living Water in the midst of the wilderness of this life. The endless frantic seizing and grasping in an attempt to satisfy our souls is brought to an end by simply coming to Jesus. That is what seeking Jesus is—the perpetual drawing near to Him.

All desires of our souls are fulfilled in Him and Him alone. This is the communication of Psalm 63. All the desires of my being—all the thirsts of my soul—cannot be quenched by anything other than God Himself. God alone, His presence, His Word, and His will fulfill our inward cravings. Jesus showed us that the initial drink becomes an endless drinking when He causes the rivers of living water to flow inside us. We can expect not only to be filled, but also to be able to drink our fill from this confluence inside us. That is the image that Jesus gave to us of a life that receives the Spirit—an endless well of fellowship that quenches our cravings. Jesus says in John 4:14 (NKJV), *"But whoever drinks of the water that I shall give him will never thirst. But the water that I shall give him will become in him a fountain of water springing up into everlasting life."* No wonder *holiness is the fruit of being addicted to the maximum pleasure of life, which is God Himself.*

We must drink. *No amount of outward contact with the river will quench the inward thirst of the soul.* We must come to Him ourselves and not be content to be around individuals who are satisfied with God. If we want eternal fruit that is significant to God, then we must come to Him, delight in Him, and our enjoyment of Him will cause our interests in worthless things to wither away as we will know by experience that He is inexhaustibly the satisfaction of our souls.

CHAPTER 3

Earnestly I Seek You

You, God, are my God, earnestly I seek you

(Psalm 63:1 NIV).

A professor of mine in Bible college, Dr. Robert Gladstone, once told us, "Worship is the soul's attempt to quench its thirst." One can worship anything, for we can set our inward gaze upon whatever we wish. This is our individuality, the freedom to choose God or not, which is the game of love. Oh, how He longs for our love.

Though many profess God in the public place, God is only worshipped and adored truly by those who seek Him in the private place. Our musician, full of the rich, tangible presence of God, says, *"You, God, are my God; earnestly I seek You."* To seek God is to intentionally set our wills upon Him. God is only our God when He is our pursuit. To not seek Him is to reject Him as God. To not seek Him is to seek something else. The resolution to set the inward gaze of our soul upon God in earnestness and sober diligence is the only true worship of God. *His presence, His person, His voice, His Word, and His will are our source of life, objective of life, and joy of life.*

Oh, to keep before us the simple truth that His will is in His presence and His presence is in His will! Such a submission to God is entrance into a glorious experience of God. An experience in which is not only satisfaction, but also at times rapturous delight that can even overflow in the soul to such degree that the physical body can be affected. David stated, *"My flesh longs for You."* Have you had such an experience? The bliss of His presence so overwhelming that your physical body feels a sort of heavenly delight? Such wondrous heavenly glories, regardless of the tribulations of life, are our lot. The bliss of drugs, sex, and pleasures in this world that turn men out of their minds are so far inferior to the ecstasy we experience in God. These other things are all counterfeits of the glory of God's person satisfying the soul through direct contact with Him. Because man doesn't realize that he was made to live united with God through surrender to Him, he seeks out pleasures for himself outside of God. Herein is the self-life that keeps men bound in misery and emptiness.

Heaven seeps its way into the earth through the lives of those who seem to experience Heaven while on the earth. Charles Spurgeon said that Robert Chapman was "the saintliest man [he] ever knew."[5] I believe the reason is found in the words of Robert Chapman's friend John Nelson Darby, "We talk of the heavenliness, but Robert Chapman lives in them."[6] To live a satisfied, peaceful life is a result of experiencing the bliss that God is. Such a life is the representation of the salvation that He offers to the world in Christ.

Anyone can tell me it is raining outside, but a man drenched with water as he walks into a room is dripping with the substance of his testimony. The Christian who lives satisfied with God testifies to the world that God is enough. The Christian who doesn't live satisfied with God testifies to the world that God is *not* enough.

An old saintly woman was asked, "What is this gospel that you believe, and how do you believe it?" Her reply is rest and joy itself: "God is satisfied with His Son—that is the gospel I believe. I am satisfied with Him, too—that is how I believe it."

CHAPTER 4

Always Needing Him

I thirst for you, my whole being longs for you
(Psalm 63:1 NIV).

The soul thirsts for God. The word *thirst* is the perfect term to capture both desire and need. God Himself is the soul's greatest need and desire. Those who recognize Him humble themselves and cry, "My soul thirsts for You."

Apart from submission to God's Spirit, the soul is a fountain of wickedness, restive, rebellious, and unmanageable, crying out in desperate thirst for satisfaction. Endless attempts are constantly being made among humanity to excel and attain heights and depths to satisfy what the heart and mind thirsts for. And what many fail to realize through their whole sojourning upon the earth is that satisfaction for the soul apart from submission to God is simply not possible.

Relationships and romantic ideas of life are tirelessly pursued in an attempt to quench the burning thirst inside man's affections. But it is simply not possible. The man after God's own heart states, "My soul thirsts for You." The recognition in his spiritual life is that only the person of God—namely, His presence and voice—can extinguish the flickering, crazed scramble of the soul.

Beloved, we need God. We will always need Him. He is an infinite ocean-depth of happy rest. He is the endless wellspring of life, the inexhaustible Source. He is the constant bliss, joy, and peace of being. Without His presence, the soul extends itself toward other things, lesser things, things that can never satisfy, and if they are tolerated, they will inflict great damage.

CHAPTER 5

Bread and Life

Man shall not live by bread alone, but by every word that proceeds from the mouth of God

(Matthew 4:4 NKJV).

For many Christians, their most sensible experience of God was stumbled upon during an extreme situation that caused them to press through into an unprecedented place of peace and rest. Yet others point back to an incredible moment where God used someone (as God loves to do) to bring the dew of Heaven into their lives. But experiencing God doesn't only happen when another believer is around, or in times of trouble, or while praying for breakthrough. Rather, experiencing God should happen daily. In fact, a daily experience of God is essential to life itself for believers.

In Matthew 4:4, Jesus likened God's words presently spoken to bread, to our source of life. Notice the text doesn't say, "by every word that proceeded out of the mouth of God." No, it says, *"by every word that proceeds out of the mouth of God."* His spoken words are still living and still speaking because they are *"spirit and life"* (John 6:33 NKJV). Christ speaks Himself. Or another way to say it is He dispenses Himself by speaking.

The receptivity of God's voice is the most transformative phenomenon. This is one of the many reasons His voice is so precious. When He is speaking to us, He is giving Himself to us. Such is a delight that the world cannot know or match. "One hour with God infinitely exceeds all the pleasures and delights of this lower world," said David Brainerd, missionary to the Delaware tribe.[7]

What we have in the gospel is God Himself. Is there anything or anyone that can be compared with God? The man of prayer realizes this and believes this and experiences this. He runs to God as his refuge, help, and strength as well as his pleasure, joy, and bliss. How wonderfully brilliant of God to make what is most important easiest and what is our greatest need our greatest delight so that we can easily find Him as refuge and delightfully find Him to be everything we need.

God's desire is to be your greatest desire. His greatest delight is to be all your delight. One of my Bible school professors rephrased a line from the Westminster Confession as, "The chief end of man is to glorify God by finding pleasure in Him."

CHAPTER 6

Feeling God

Whom having not seen you love. Though now you do not see Him, yet believing, you rejoice with joy inexpressible and full of glory

(1 Peter 1:8 NKJV).

One of the most common questions that I receive is, "Why don't I feel God?" Yet we have all been counseled at one time or another with the statement, "We cannot go by what we feel," or "We must put faith over feelings." But is this true? Should we be so indifferent to whether we "feel" God that it does not matter either way? Do we just soldier on without a wonder of whether we have what we profess? Should we be so disconnected from "feeling" His presence that we present the experience of God as a lottery?

Growing up in the Church has wearied me of mere professions and confessions. How do we know that we are His? Is it not by the Spirit? Is it not the abiding of the Spirit in our hearts? Is it not a bearing witness with my Spirit that I am a child of God? Is there no joy or peace or satisfaction in Christ? Does the Scripture promise me a joy that I cannot feel? A peace that I cannot feel? A love that I cannot feel? A satisfaction that I cannot feel? Charles Spurgeon once noted, "Only a corpse is without feeling." He went on to note that "to be unfeeling is to be unfruitful."

Maybe the question is not whether we should feel God, but rather *what does it mean to feel God?* It is nonnegotiable that we do not live based on our human desires and emotions, but it is equally true that the new life we have in Christ is evidenced by new sensible feelings, emotions, and desires. The inability to sense God was our fallen state. Being born again is to be delivered from our dependency upon and submission to our carnal feelings. Being born again means we have a new faculty implanted in the soul that can perceive God. It is not only an astonishing reality of feeling, but also the means by which He now governs our lives through His Spirit and Word. The Spirit is not merely claimed but felt. The Word is not merely cerebrally accepted but felt in the inward being even as the Spirit bears with our spirit that we are children of God.

A dictionary defines *feeling* as "an emotional state or reaction." Does He who dropped out of Heaven by the weight of love feel nothing of me? Do I who know what He lived and died for me feel nothing for Him? Does what He has done for me cause no rise in emotion? To use an analogy, imagine I brought what looked like a firearm into a service, and I told the congregation that it was a water pistol. The congregation would note what it was and fearlessly remain seated. But if I told them and showed them that it was a real firearm, their hearts would palpitate, and many would leave. Few would even dare to come near me as I held it. The reason is simple, what you believe determines much of how you feel. To believe it was a water pistol was to know that, no matter how real it looked, it was fake and could only wet a person with fluid. But to see that the gun was real and to believe it to be so would shake people up. So it is with this precious book that we have in the Bible. To read it as *The Chronicles of Narnia* or *The Lord of the Rings* may causes a stimulation in the imagination at best. But to read the Bible and believe it is to feel sins forgiven, to expect the clouds to break open. It is to realize victory over sin and the fellowship of the Spirit. For us who have the gift of faith from Christ, to believe the Word is the highest emotion anyone can feel.

Looking into the life of Jesus, we see that He did nothing apart from the empowerment of spiritual perception of His Father. Perception is defined as the ability to see, or hear or sense. Paul actually prayed for the

Ephesians to have the eyes of their hearts opened (see Ephesians 1:18). Jesus told those who had been given ears to hear to use them and *"hear what the Spirit says to the churches"* (Revelation 2:7 NKJV). Our new man has perception of God, sense of God, and feelings for God.

The sense of God is not just important; it is our source of spiritual empowerment. It means that the soul believes. Romans 15:13 (NKJV) says, *"Now may the God of hope fill you with all joy and peace in believing, that you will abound in hope by the power of the Holy Spirit."* Our spiritual "feeling," as stated in 1 Peter 1:8, is love and joy in our believing in Him, yet not seeing Him.

Yes, this is our portion under His rule. Even though we don't physically see Him, we experience Him, in joy and glory. *We don't see Him physically, but we perceive Him spiritually.* Moses endured *"seeing Him who is unseen"* (Hebrews 11:27 AMP). The early Christian writers spoke of the "imageless vision." Faith is *"substance"*; faith is *"evidence"* (Hebrews 11:1 NKJV). It is just not in the physical world to be seen. It is perceived so true that it is expected.

Feeling rightly understood as a spiritual perceptibility in the Scriptures simply means *peace that passes all understanding*, as Philippians 4:7 (NKJV) describes it, *"And the peace of God, which surpasses all understanding, will guard your hearts and minds through Christ Jesus."* This reality of God that far exceeds mathematics is the life source and guidance of those whose minds and hearts are stayed upon Him. It is far beyond the cerebral. It is spiritual.

Peace enjoyed and beyond comprehension. What does this mean? Well, maybe it could be better seen as this: It makes absolutely no sense to have peace right now, but I do. Such wonderful peace acts as a guard for your mind and your heart. God's protection over your heart and mind is the experience of His presence that blissfully numbs our souls to doubt, fear, reason, questions, etc. Our only job is to look at Him. Isaiah 26:3 (NKJV) tells us, *"You will keep him in perfect peace whose mind is stayed on You...."*

Feeling is inseparable from experience. Should we experience God every time we pray? The New Covenant answer is always the same, "Yes!" Without experience, it is simply not communion with a person.

If Christianity is without feelings and sensibility, then Scripture, Christ, the prophets, and the psalmist are all participating in a delusion. Jesus said, *"That which is born of the flesh is flesh, and that which is born of the Spirit is spirit"* (John 3:6 NKJV). Saints live in a new system of existence that is dependent upon a living person who palpitates life into our being through faith in Him that is expressed in ceaseless prayer. Puritan theologian and author Richard Baxter wrote, "Prayer is the breath of the New Creation."[8]

A. W. Tozer wrote, "It cannot but be a major in the life of any man to live in a church from childhood to old age with nothing more real than some synthetic god compounded of theology and logic, but having no eyes to see and no heart to love."[9] The terrible indictment against the Church is that we have substituted logic for life. Jesus condemned the Pharisees not because of their lack of knowing the text of the Scriptures but because they had no idea what the living God was actually saying. They had no living experience of God's person.

Feeling God, experiencing God, is not an option or perk of His presence. It is rather the means by which He frees us and empowers us to be able to obey Him. It is simply the consciousness of our Christ-wrought union with Him. The experience of God is the enjoyment of the New Covenant, the Covenant in which God Himself would make His abode in us. Jesus says in John 14:23 (NKJV), *"If anyone loves Me, he will keep My word; and My Father will love him, and We will come to him and make Our home with him."* Dear reader, if you have lived your Christian life denying dependance on logic, sight, and feelings, you have done well. But if that is where it ends, you have stopped too short. Enter into the spiritual life where we see, hear, feel, and experience God Himself and life by such blissful fellowship.

CHAPTER 7

The Soul at Home

The grace of the Lord Jesus Christ, and the love of God, and the communion of the Holy Spirit be with you all. Amen
                                    (2 Corinthians 13:14 NKJV).

I ask you, dear reader, in all honesty, can you say the life that you live is animated by a daily, delightful exchange with God? Is the person of Christ a real and present experience in your reading of the Scriptures? Is communion with God the source of your life? Is your soul at home in His presence?

A friend of mine once asked me, "How do people pray for hours on end? I pray for five minutes and have nothing more to say." I submit to you, as I did to my friend, that the first mistake in this question is the assumption that prayer is words. To think that prayer is words is like thinking love is a hug. Love can be expressed through a hug, but love is a far deeper reality. Words are an expression of prayer, but prayer is much deeper. If words were prayer, then Paul would have been encouraging the life of a jabberer when he wrote, *"Pray without ceasing"* (1 Thessalonians 5:17 NKJV). Though prayer can be an endless, uninterrupted exchange and interaction with God, *prayer is simply the soul's fixation upon God.*

When the disciples asked Jesus to teach them to pray, Jesus said, *"When you pray, say…"* (Luke 11:2 NKJV). Jesus established the state of prayer before speaking. Prayer, then, is the state of the heart. "Prayer is the application of the heart to God, and the internal exercise of love," wrote Madame Guyon, author and French mystic.[10] Or as Richard Baxter, the English Puritan church leader and theologian penned, "Prayer is the breath of the new creature. The spirit of adoption given to every child of God is a spirit of prayer."[11] It's "the nearest approach to God, and the highest enjoyment of Him, that we are capable of in this life," said William Law, English devotional writer and mystic.[12] *Prayer is conscious union with God. It's the soul at home with Him.*

So, one may ask in response, "That's wonderful that prayer is that way for you, but what about me? I want that, but reading the Bible is like unwanted math homework, and praying is as boring as a middle school lecture." *Dear saint, the utmost purpose of the sending of the Spirit into our hearts is for you and me to enjoy union and communion with God and, from there, to proclaim Him in and through our lives.* What is the Christian life if it isn't lived in His presence through unbroken communion?

Charles Spurgeon inspires us toward communion with these words he offered from the Puritan preacher and author Thomas Brooks:

> Believer, you cannot have too frequent communion with God, or too frequent intercourse with Jesus. You cannot have your heart too frequently filled with joy unspeakable, and full of glory, and with that peace which passes understanding. You cannot have heaven too often brought down into your hearts, or your hearts too often carried up to heaven, and therefore you cannot be too frequent in closet prayer.[13]

I encourage you to cast yourself completely in prayer and say, "Lord, I don't want to live a life unacquainted with the delight of Your presence through Your Holy Spirit. Help my soul to be at home in prayer and communion with You."

CHAPTER 8

His Call to Relief and Rest

Come to Me, all you who labor and are heavy laden, and I will give you rest

(Matthew 11:28 NKJV).

Such an invitation from the mouth of Christ, God's perfect expression, carries a beauty that stands as one of the most comforting statements we find in the Scriptures. The fact that this invitation is extended to all is a wonderful expression of God's kindness and love, for He will never reject anyone who will come to Him (see John 6:37). The more we experience Him, the more this universal and continual invitation allures us and causes all our worthless interests to wither away. Personally, Jesus says to me every day of my life, *"Come to Me."*

This phrase in its most basic understanding means entering Jesus' presence. It means leaving everything else behind, both our failures and our victories. It means leaving our own way and coming to Him. It does not mean coming to a method or a practice. *Coming to Jesus means coming to a living person.* It means looking unto Him, giving Him all our attention.

Jesus calls to everyone who is suffering under the weariness and heaviness of life to look only to Him for relief and rest. This invitation to come to Him reveals that our weariness in this life has its roots in the lack of His presence and our heaviness in self-reliance. A life of continually finding rest from life's fears, worries, pains, strivings, sin, and oppression can only be a life of continually coming to Jesus.

The presence of Jesus frees us from the constant stress that the tick of time puts upon our souls; this is called rest. The presence of Jesus frees us from the constant frustration of that "need to have" that brews in our souls; this is called rest. Our senses are constantly bombarded by our surroundings, but the presence of Jesus frees us from their influence; this is called rest. In the presence of Jesus, we are free from striving, and we see God; this is called rest.

Rest is the ceasing of natural activity and the ignition of divine activity. The life of rest is the life empowered by God. "We can have no power from Christ unless we live in a persuasion that we have none of our own," said John Owen, Puritan theologian, reformer, and preacher.[14] *"For it is God who works in you both to will and to do for His good pleasure,"* wrote the apostle Paul in Philippians 2:13 (NKJV). And Jesus says in John 14:10 (NASB1995), *"The Father abiding in Me does His works."*

CHAPTER 9

Easy and Light

*Take My yoke upon you and learn from Me, for I am gentle
and lowly in heart, and you will find rest for your souls. For
My yoke is easy and My burden is light*
(Matthew 11:29-30 NKJV).

The heavenly blissful rest, enjoyment, and freedom in God's presence
are a promise. Jesus died for our sins and closed the distance between us
and God. It is the work of the cross that makes His conscious presence
our current, unchanging, privileged possession.

In the next breath, He who said, *"Come to Me,"* said, *"Take My yoke
upon you."* That yoke can also be understood to be kindness. *We drop the
yoke of works and pick up the sweet character of the Lord.* We switch from
works to knowing Him. To know Him is better than all the works of
human ingenuity.

Throughout the Gospels, Jesus constantly taught the fundamental
Kingdom reality that He is our liberation. At the core of this freedom is
being rescued from the tyranny of self-rule. We were not made to rule
ourselves. *Our self-management is too feeble, too flawed, and too flimsy to
sustain us.* If man is left to himself, he destroys himself because the natural inclination of man is sin, and sin leads to death. Many scholars believe
that what Jesus was referring to as a yoke is the teaching of a rabbi. If
Jesus is our Rabbi, we receive His rule and way. His rule contains only
that which He is Himself—joy, peace, power, wisdom, life, etc. His yoke

is His wonderful rule, and it is far lighter than any other. As author Dane Ortlund in his book *Gentle and Lowly* wrote, "His yoke is kind and his burden is light. That is, his yoke is a nonyoke, and his burden a nonburden. What helium does to a balloon, Jesus' yoke does to his followers."[15]

Jesus also used the word *easy* to describe His yoke. No matter what is happening to us, we can find divine ease when we come into His presence and yield to His dominion, simply because He will carry every load. Even in the heart of suffering, there is a fellowship with Him that gives us *"the peace of God, which surpasses all understanding"* (Philippians 4:7 NKJV). This means that He promises to give us peace when it doesn't make any natural sense. It's the peace that passes the ability to be understood.

When we come to Jesus and take up His light burden and easy yoke, our hearts learn of His meekness and humility. Could it be that learning Christ's humility, gentleness, and meekness is liberty from heaviness and straining? The taking up of His yoke, or shall I say it more clearly, the renunciation of our own self-rule and the submission to Him are humility and meekness. There isn't a more unshackled life than the one who comes to Jesus and learns of Him.

Remember this: It is not the yoke of God that is heavy. The weight belongs to our sin and self-management. We often try to wear a crown made for God and wonder why it is too heavy for our heads. Selfishness and pride wear out the saints and lead humanity captive. *Independence and self-sufficiency weigh us down as we drag the heavy yoke of the self-life.* Stubbornness causes us to reject Christ's easy yoke. The one who will not renounce self will never come to Jesus. Mark my words, the self-sufficient one will die of fatigue.

Praise God! Jesus has called for any and all to come to Him and enter His presence to find this God-ordained realm of rest. Let us humble ourselves and come to Jesus every day. Here we lay down our heavy yokes and pick up His easy one. Here we take our restless, weary, burdened, and heavy souls, and He gives us rest and ease in return in His presence. I can't think of a better summary than the eloquence of Spurgeon: "The yoke will be no more a burden to us than wings are to a bird, or her wedding-ring is to a bride."[16]

CHAPTER 10

Rest—The Realm of Perception

There remains therefore a rest for the people of God. For he who has entered His rest has himself also ceased from his works as God did from His

(Hebrews 4:9-10 NKJV).

There is a rest that isn't mere deep breaths and relaxation but rather the relinquishing of our own efforts. It has often been said, "Faith can be spelled R.E.S.T." This rest-trust in God makes perception of Him possible. I once heard an old saint say, "Overstimulation kills the receptivity of the soul." The inverse is also true—*rest opens our receptivity of Him.*

I constantly need to remind myself of this works-dissolving fact that Spurgeon said: "You stand before God as accepted as Christ is accepted: and…you are as dear to God as Christ is dear, and as accepted in the righteousness of Christ as Christ is accepted in his own obedience."[17] That is rest.

So often I have fallen into a striving that seeks to break something open, and I have failed to enjoy what Jesus has broken open, namely, the veil between us and God (see Hebrews 10:19-20). It does me well to keep before my eyes the old exhortation of preacher and storyteller Arthur Burt, "Snuggle, don't struggle." A better summary of our bridal union with Christ I cannot find. I am not negating the scriptural truths of running to win, wrestling against, or enduring as a soldier (see 1 Corinthians 9:24; Ephesians 6:12; 2 Timothy 2:3). Each of these have a place in our earthly sojourn, but none of these analogies refer to our experience of the presence of God. They simply cannot be applied to the blissful communion we have with Christ in the gospel. That, my precious reader, is a gift (see Acts 10:45). Not only is it undeserved, it cannot be earned. It is simply received.

Restored fellowship with God is the cream of the goodness of the good news. By faith in Christ, we receive what He deserves, because He bore what we deserved. That is the rest to which I am referring; that quiet trust in Christ is our only means of receiving from God.

That rest granted to us by faith in Christ is why I believe the exhortation, "Snuggle, don't struggle," is the sum of victorious Christianity. *Our Christ-wrought access to God ends all struggling and gives us the intimate privilege of snuggling, hidden in His bosom, captured by His charms, and enraptured in His arms.* If we lay our heads upon His breast, we gain access to the divine treasure chest. In this treasure chest are all the riches of Christ Himself (see Colossians 2:3). The riches of Christ that we receive *"through the knowledge of Him"* are all that we need for *"life and godliness"* (2 Peter 1:3 NKJV). The glorious gospel gives us rest. As the lines of this poem so eloquently attest:

> He came His arm around me;
> I leaned upon His chest;
> I did not long to feel more strong
> So sweet the childlike rest.
> —Poem written by Miss Havergal, quoted on page 267 of
> Flowers from a Puritan's Garden by C.H. Spurgeon

In the gospel, we are lifted and carried by Him. This rest-trust in Christ is the antithesis of human effort. As F. B. Meyer exhorts us, in all circumstances of life, "Remind God of His entire responsibility."[18] No man can boast of anything when he realizes that his Christian life is by God's grace through faith in Him. This is not of ourselves. Salvific rest is a ceasing of striving and a casting of oneself upon God's mercy. By faith in the gospel, we quickly realize that our need isn't to be self-strong, but to be still. The former obstructs rather than encourages a life of experiential union with God.

Rest is simply this—the soul giving God His proper place. This rest is brilliantly described in a paragraph from Spurgeon's sermon notes:

> The Puritans speak of faith as a recumbency, a leaning. It needs no power to lean; it is a cessation from our own strength, and allowing our weakness to depend upon another's power. Let no man say, "I cannot lean"; it is not a question of what you can do, but a confession of what you cannot do, and a leaving of the whole matter with Jesus.[19]

CHAPTER 11

The Embrace We Long For

And He took them up in His arms, laid His hands on them, and blessed them

(Mark 10:16 NKJV).

Dear reader, because I don't know you personally, I wonder if you have ever taken time to strip everything away and just simply sit with God? If you have, I'm sure you have recognized something about Him. All He's interested in doing is holding you close. The Church thrives in no other place.

The sweet, intimate experience of Jesus, the cooling drink of the Spirit, is a direct contact with God that satisfies the soul out of itself. *A surrendered, yielded, trusting faith experiences the embrace for which our souls are longing.* Though such an experience may come through a church meeting, a conference, a betrayal, a sickness, a loss, or a rock-bottom experience, it doesn't have to. It should be the source of our daily joy, life, peace, and strength. Nothing is more authentically transformative as laying everything else aside and simply coming to Him.

When my daughter was young, I saw her crying in her room about something. I was deeply concerned, so I walked into the room and bent down to her level and sweetly asked her, "What is wrong, baby?" She began to tell me her pressing issue. She expounded on her disturbing problem, and I picked her up, laid her head on my chest, and said, "Whenever you feel frustrated, sad, angry, confused, or hurt, or anything, you run straight to Daddy, and I'll put your head on my chest, and you can find rest. Forget about everything else and just know that I am here. I can help you. After you calm down, I can handle whatever it is." She didn't respond with anything but a deep sigh of comfort and quietness as she rested on my chest and I rubbed her back. In that moment, a communication deeper than words took place. There was an *exchange happening*. There was a transferring of my rest into her problem.

Often, we feel that what is happening in our lives is very important or troublesome, and we cry and stress. If we go straight to Him and simply lay our heads on His chest, He will be our rest. We will find that He is more important than whatever is pressing upon us.

I am afraid that we have theologically reduced God's embrace of the human soul to a symbol. Could it be that there is lifelessness in the Church today because we have failed to point people to God Himself? Could it be that we have emphasized something more than the real experience of His embrace? Could it be that a large part of our deep depravity in prayer is due to a lack of our souls receiving the embrace of God? Could it be that many Christians have a very difficult time maturing because of a lack of touch?

God is never responsible for an inconsistent experience of Him. The fault falls on our unwillingness to fall into His arms. My personal belief is that, without the embrace of God in our lives, we are quickly decaying. Charles Spurgeon wrote in the classic *Morning and Evening*, "He kills your doubts and your fears by the closeness of His embrace." Sometimes, the greatest thing God can say to us is not intelligible at all; it's simply being held. We may not know what He is saying, but we will sense what He is doing. He values the indelible more than the intelligible.

If we will allow the Spirit of God to woo us away from our sins, failures, weaknesses, performance, strivings, troubles, and trials—and into His arms—we will find rest. *Living in His rest is both the mark of maturity and the maturing work.* We must be willing to see that only He matters. We demonstrate this by leaving everything else behind.

Pray this with me, "Precious God, hold me. Drain out my inward poison. Hold me and cause competition, comparison, lust, greed, anger, offense, and frustration to dissolve in me. Hold me and give me love that I don't have, joy that I long for, peace that I need, self-control, patience, kindness, and all those things that You are."

CHAPTER 12

Alone with God

But you, when you pray, go into your room, and when you have shut your door, pray to your Father who is in the secret place

(Matthew 6:6 NKJV).

The first and most essential element to living a life focused upon Jesus is to be alone with Him. Being alone with Him cannot be overemphasized. *Living in perpetual fellowship with Him throughout the day is Christianity.* Most people, however, find this extremely difficult.

The reason is simple: The secret place is the power of the abiding place; the foundation of your life in Him in public is receiving life from Him in private. English preacher and *The Pilgrim's Progress* author John Bunyan wrote an irreplaceable key, "He who runs from God in the morning will scarcely find Him the rest of the day."

We are married to Him. Conjugal love and nuptial privileges open to us the reality that there are certain things a husband and wife will do only when they're alone together. In holy allegory, we know that there are certain things, precious things, valuable things, personal things, unifying things that Jesus will only do with you when you are alone with Him.

When Jesus taught on prayer in Matthew 6, He said, *"Go into your room."* This is separation. Leave the company of others and get alone. Then He said, *"Shut the door."* He not only wants us to separate ourselves, but He also wants us to shut out the noise. *Separation, solitude, and silence are the steroids of prayer.* They will aid your communion greatly, not only because they are helps in concentration, but because they bring us into the arena of complete honesty. God and man, alone. Jacob was alone when God touched his hip (see Genesis 32:25). Moses was alone when God revealed his goodness (see Exodus 3:6). As Art Katz, a mighty spokesman of God, said, you must "be ruthless with yourself to get alone, lock the door and seek God and be found by Him."[20]

The following are three elements of Christ's discipleship:

1. Without time there can be no discipleship. Time is our spiritual fermentation. Bible school teacher Walter H. Buettler said, "Time is the tuition in the school of the Spirit."[21]
2. What kind of time? It is time with Him, being in the presence of Jesus, which will miraculously fashion us into true followers of Jesus. South African pastor Andrew Murray said, "Christ's presence was the training of the disciples."[22]
3. What kind of being with Him? It is communicative time. Exchange and intercourse of Spirit with Him will increase into knowing Him. No one knows everything about a person in their initial meeting with them. We must spend time with them to know them. Tozer notes that "Moses used the fact that he knew God as an argument for knowing Him more."

The American Trappist monk and mystic Thomas Merton wrote, "Without solitude of some sort, there is and can be no maturity." He continued:

> There must be a time of day when the man who makes plans forgets his plans, and acts as if he had no plans at all. There must be a time of day when the man who has to speak falls very silent. And his mind forms no more propositions.... There must be a time when the man of resolutions puts aside his resolutions as if they had all been broken....[23]

The Scriptures are one complete call to come to Him—a call to be absorbed in the Holy Spirit. What does that mean? It means spending as much time with Him as your God-given responsibilities allow and abiding in Him from that separated place. Two quotes from evangelist and author Leonard Ravenhill move my heart, "You have as much of God as you want," and "To be much for God, we must be much with God." It is no wonder that he spoke such words because his mentor Samuel Chadwick taught him that "No man is greater than His prayer life."

CHAPTER 13

A Revelation of His Radiance

He was transfigured before them; and His face shone like the sun, and His garments became as white as light
(Matthew 17:2 NASB).

Have you experienced the tender alluring of the Spirit? I once read a sentence written by the great Charles G. Finney—leader in the Second Great Awakening in the United States—that startled me: "Cherish the slightest impressions of the Holy Spirit." *How we respond to the Spirit determines everything about us.* A love for Christ makes us soft toward His inclinations. The inverse is true, a hardness toward His inclinations is an indication of our desire and value of Him. How we respond to His impressions reveals what He means to us. For when we cherish those slight impressions, we cherish God Himself. Whenever you are alone and sense the sweetness of His nearness, it is good to remind yourself that what you are sensing in the nearness and reality of God Himself.

In Matthew 17, we see Jesus drew three men up the mountain. A separation with Him amid their separation unto Him. He set these three men apart for a unique "seeing" of Him. He raised their understanding of Him by revelation of Himself. This was so effective that, when Peter at the end of his days wrote his letter to the church, he recalled this moment and said that he had his hope made surer because he had seen

Jesus transfigured on that day. In the same way that Peter was transformed by the sight of Jesus, Jesus wants to raise our lives above the earth through a revelation of the radiance of His person.

Christ always leads us into a revelation of Himself, for God has nothing more precious to offer us than His own person. All who followed Jesus had a revelation of Him, but those who followed Him up onto the mountain of communion had a greater revelation of Him. Here is the desire of Christ that we would pass the initial revelation of Him into a grander vision of Him. He is so happy to show Himself to us yet yearns to reveal even more of Himself. It is interesting to note the way that this revelation came. Take note that, when Jesus revealed Himself to these disciples, they heard God the Father's voice. Maybe we can note that, *in the presence of the Son, we hear the Father, and through the speaking of the Father, we see the Son.* The Father confirms the Son and says, *"Listen to Him!"* (Matthew 17:5 AMP). This doesn't just mean, "Do what He says." It also means *give all your life's attention to the Son.*

Here lies the major issue: We have given our life's attention to other things. Perhaps we have looked intently at the brightness of His clothes, the hovering glory cloud, or even the appearance of Moses and Elijah. But God, while not diminishing the by-products of His manifest glory, pinpoints the prime element of the glory of God—Jesus Himself. Though all these manifestations are from Christ and cannot be found apart from Him, He Himself deserves all our focus. A spiritually wise person understands that the presence of Jesus is the most excellent of all.

In response to the Son's breathtaking unveiling and the Father's thunderous speaking, the disciples fall on their faces. Is there a better picture of humbling ourselves before God? *Humility is the only right response to seeing the glory and hearing the voice of God, for its origin was, is, and always will be, in a vision of Jesus.* Charles Spurgeon reminds us in his little book *Barbed Arrows*, "A vision of God is the quietus of pride."

Oh dear friend, God is drawn to humility and humility happens at the sight of Him. *"And Jesus came to them and touched them and said, 'Get up, and do not be afraid.' And raising their eyes, they saw no one except Jesus Himself alone"* (Matthew 17:7-8 NASB).

When they lifted up their eyes they *saw nothing else but Jesus alone.* They had followed Him up the mountain. They saw His glorious person. They fell in humility before God. They then saw only Jesus. *Such is the result of following Him—we see Him.* In seeing Him, we are humbled before Him. Humility sees only Him. It doesn't take note of others or itself, only Him. This is the result of the vision of Jesus.

CHAPTER 14

The Password That Unlocks His Heart

My soul longs, yes, even faints for the courts of the Lord; my heart and my flesh cry out for the living God
(Psalm 84:2 NKJV).

Once I was taken into a vision and saw a door with a divine light at the end of a long, dark alley. The light was shining out from the bottom and side cracks. I knew Heaven was behind this door, and I was full of excitement to walk through it. When I tried to enter, though, it was locked. So, I knocked. Out of the top of the door, a little slit opened up, and I could see eyes looking at me through the door. This man was smiling. I could tell from the look of His eyes that He was happy to see me. I knew it was the Lord. He said to me, "What is the password?"

Immediately, I panicked because I had no idea. I thought quickly to myself, *Is it a Scripture? A name? A song?* I had no idea. I felt helpless and hopeless. I was silent for a long minute. I felt He would shut the slit, and I would not be able to come in if I didn't get the password right; I felt that I should have known this. *Maybe He told me, and I forgot?* I questioned myself. I was deflated completely. As a grasping effort, hoping to pull on the mercy in His heart, I blurted out, "I only want You, Lord!" Immediately, the door was unlocked, and the sound of it knocked me out of the vision, and I was back in my prayer chair.

This vision taught me so much. It is not knowledge that draws Him to us. It is not the right song or the secret mysteries that mean anything to Him. He is simply looking for that one who only wants Him. It is that one who finds in Him everything that they could ever desire. *As long as other things are looked to, we cannot see Him.*

Sex, perversions, drugs, a husband or a wife, kids, money, a dream job, fame or even power, miracles, success, a platform, knowledge, or wonders cannot begin to scratch the surface of what it is to have Jesus as life and pleasure. His presence and person are the satisfaction of our souls. It is knowing Him that is the sweet empowering bliss of life.

CHAPTER 15

Yielding into Adoration

Be still, and know that I am God

(Psalm 46:10 NKJV).

One of the first keys to experiencing intimacy with Jesus is understanding the intimate words in Song of Solomon, *"Let him kiss me"* (Song of Solomon 1:2 NKJV). Yielding is the secret, the ceasing of efforts and our still surrender in adoration. Let us yield to Him with no agenda but to let Him hold us.

Can we be so simple as to trust Him to perform His work as we sit quiet in adoration, casting all helplessly upon Him. Can we yield until our spiritual eyes see the rivers of His refreshing glistening with the light of His countenance? Can we yield to no other end than to be yielded, and remain? This is where the kiss is. Madame Guyon, one of the leading mystics of the Quietist movement, wrote:

> When you are quiet before God, simply allow yourself time to enjoy His presence and be filled full in your spirit.... Hearing is a passive rather than an active procedure. Rest. Rest. Rest in God's love. Simply listen and be attentive to God. These passive actions will permit God to communicate His love to you.... When your spirit is centered on God all activities He

initiates will be full of peace and natural and so spontaneous that it will appear to you that there has hardly been any activity at all.[24]

Often, we cannot hear God or experience His heart simply because our hearts are not willing to yield enough to wait for God. The sad fact is, for many of us, His presence is no longer the purpose of prayer. Waiting is yielding to God by taking the time to give Him all our attention. It's a *turning* of our attention, if you will. When you turn and sustain your gaze wholeheartedly in adoration upon God, little by little your soul will begin to detach from the cares of this world. It will release your heart from self-consciousness and dissolve the "itch of efforts" and the "frenzy of need."

In giving God all our attention, we become quiet *and* still. *Quietness is the absence of external noise. Stillness is the absence of internal noise.* So many people become quiet in their surroundings but are filled with noise internally; thus, they have no stillness. Our need is not to merely be quiet, but to *be still.* What we really need so as to hear the Lord is to remove ourselves from the hurricane outside *and* to silence the clatter inside.

At this point, His presence will begin to be sensible. By this I mean a sense of sweet tranquility that moves throughout your being, as a direct result of your soul yielding to the Spirit. Without His presence, we will get tired of waiting, because we must understand that we do not wait *for* His presence but *in* His presence. We must note that, in these moments of yielding in His presence, the purpose of prayer is being accomplished. Here we resign ourselves to linger, content with Him alone. This is what I wish someone would have told me at the very beginning of my fellowship with God.

Lingering is gazing upon Him by sustaining all our attention upon Him. Soon, the clutter clears, and we can hear, perceive, know, or often find contentment with Him. The bliss of His presence is found in the enjoyment of waiting upon Him.

When we wait on the Lord, it pulls the Word to us. David said, *"I wait for Your word"* (Psalm 119:74 NASB). In other words, the *word* comes through *waiting*. If we would take time to simply wait on Him, we would receive His Word, experience His heart, and see His speaking through various means, the richest of which is unearthed by meditation upon the Scriptures.

Impatience is often the very thing that steals our attention and doesn't allow us to wait on the Lord. *Impatience is an idol factory*. If we don't want to wait on God, and we decide to go do *something else,* we are putting something else in His place. Remember when Moses went to the mountain and Israel became restless? They fashioned an idol in His place, and they even named the idol "Yahweh" (see Exodus 32:4-5). You can name your idol whatever you'd like. You can name it something spiritual or positive sounding. It matters not. It is still an object that is wrongfully taking the place of God. It's simple: If the origin is off, the whole thing is off. If we don't want to wait for the operation of God's Spirit, we are left with human effort and ingenuity. Oh, to live prioritizing that Holy Dove that ascended on Christ who waited and refused to move on without Him. *Impatience is disinterest in the Dove.*

Oh, the danger of allowing busyness to eliminate the simple tranquility of *waiting*. If we choose not to wait and be still, we are actually saying to the Lord, "I've got this. I don't need You to rule me. I'll go forward saying all the right things and sounding the part, but I don't need Your actual reign in my life." However, when we wait upon Him, we give Him His proper throne in our hearts.

If someone is trying to lead us or communicate to us, our attention is most important. If our attention is not fully given to the leader or communicator by listening, by looking, and by concentrating, their attempt to communicate to us will not be received in wholeness because we are divided. Keeping our attention upon God is how we can be led by Him. *What we do when God seems silent is the greatest revealer of what really has our affection and our attention.*

Our relationship with God hinges upon our attentiveness and wholehearted fixation upon His person and presence. No matter how subtle it may seem in the moment or how meaningless, it is in our looking and in our listening that we find the very source Himself. The subtle impressions of His presence will increase into ecstatic blissful currents if we refuse to irreverently move past them. I have to remind myself that the precious love exchange with God is often right behind the things I want from Him if I will refuse to let them take my attention away from Him.

This love fountain will numb the soul to unbelief, questions, the itch to do, the craving to be noticed, the lusts of the soul, and even the body's longings. This internal bliss is needed to make us more like Him. Such experiential communion brings us into the experience of our individual union with God that Christ has given to us.

Living a life in intimate communion with God is life's greatest joy, peace, satisfaction, success, and pleasure, whether we preach to millions or change tires.

CHAPTER 16

Four Keys to Aid in Abiding

Jesus answered and said to him, "If anyone loves Me, he will keep My word; and My Father will love him, and We will come to him and make Our home with him"
(John 14:23 NKJV).

There are four short keys that I believe will aid us in abiding in His presence, the first of which is *living for His presence*. We must wake up every day and remember that this day has been given to us, above all things, to enjoy our God. No matter what task is standing before us, we must adjust our soul's disposition to see that our first priority is to live for His presence. George Muller wrote, "The first great and primary business to which I ought to attend every day was, to have my soul happy in the Lord."[25]

The second key is to *live in His presence*. We must consciously abide in that inner place where the Spirit's presence is known and experienced. To do this, we must live a collected life. *The major attack upon the abiding place is scatteredness.* The devil knows that if he can scatter your soul, it will not be *still* enough to plug into the socket of life. It will remain too self-conscious to become God-conscious. Our job is to simply plug into the wall. God's job is the infusion of power.

Infusion is when the properties of one become useful in another. It is when two different things become one. To live in His presence, we must remain settled in Him by worship and surrender. If we feel the scattering of the soul, we must turn within by worship and surrender till the soul is stilled and plugged into the infusion of His Spirit in our spirit—the residence of divine glory. Madame Guyon said, "When at any time the passions are turbulent, a gentle retreat inwards unto a Present God, easily deadens and pacifies them; and any other way of contending with them rather irritates than appeases them."[26]

The third key is to *live around His presence*. I suggest this to mean that we make every decision of our lives, moments, and days around the fact that we are living for, in, and by His presence. How many things that are eating our lives away on a daily basis would be set to the side if we looked at every decision in life from the desire to maximize our reception of God? This may strike you as a bit merciless, but it drives the point home with one hard wallop. Revivalist preacher Jonathan Edwards resolved to "never do anything [he] would be afraid to do if it were the last hour of [his] life."

The fourth key is to *live from His presence*. Our counsel, words, preaching, life, and presence will carry life if they issue from a life that is living in the presence of God. We must remain in His presence, consciously and experientially, and allow everything that we are to flow from that river within. If we make Him our fountain, then He shall flow through every stream.

Because of God's call upon my life to bring the Church into a deeper experience with the life of God, I am constantly criticized as a "sunshine and rainbows" preacher. Ministers who are older, wiser, and more constant in the faith than myself have come up to me and said, "There is coming a day when God will leave you to yourself and the enemy, and there you will find out what you are truly made of." One older saint said to my father when they saw the burning love the Spirit poured out in my soul at the beginning, "He will come down with the rest of us after a while." Perhaps they are right. At the time of this writing, I am thirty years in the Lord, and maybe I am too young and naïve to understand "abandonment" times. But all I know and preach is that He *"prepare[s] a table before me in the presence of my enemies"* (Psalm 23:5 NKJV).

No matter what surrounds me, I can have sweet communion with Him. If He had to leave me to test me, then that would mean that He was seeking to fashion me into something apart from Himself. If the gospel is that He would afterward abandon me to see if I can make it on the power of human resolve apart from dependency on Him, apart from His empowering presence, then it would not be a gospel of union with God.

I heard an old saint preach that if a Christian cannot find comfort in God in his darkest hour, then the gospel and the Spirit are a farce. I don't buy it. I need Him and the sweet meals He prepares for me right in front of an enormous army of devils salivating for my soul.

He *"anoint[s] my head with oil,"* smearing His own substance upon me (Psalm 23:5 NKJV). The dripping of His oil and the fragrance of His ointment are continually upon us. Notice that *the anointing follows the table*; we eat of Him, receiving Him internally, and then He rests upon us externally. I once heard an amazing man of God say that the presence of the Lord is internal while the anointing of the Lord is external. David expounded upon this with the next statement, *"My cup runs over"* (Psalm 23:5 NKJV). When the presence of the Lord fills the inner man, it will begin to spill over and onto the outer man, just like a cup that is being filled when it overflows the sides and covers the outside. This Shepherd is so good! He lets us rest, drink, wash, eat, and then He overflows in us. The inflow creates overflow, which creates an outflow.

CHAPTER 17

What Christ Holds Dear

Put my tears into Your bottle; are they not in Your book?
(Psalm 56:8 NKJV)

If there is a room in the corridors of glory, in which Christ collects things precious to His heart, I am most certain that He has not gathered sermons, testimonies, or snapshots of a man's ministry highlights. If Christ were to take me by the hand into that precious room, He might take me to a trenching shovel. I might look at Him and say, "What is this?" To which He would smile and reply, "This is the shovel upon which your tears fell as you worshipped Me in the heat of the day without one ministry opportunity, without any personal ambition but to love Me. Do you remember? I remember."

I believe God has placed value upon things that seem insignificant to mankind. It seems that He will establish those who give themselves so completely over to Him that they are no longer concerned with ever being established at all. *He holds precious to His heart a life of intimate communion with Him that seeks nothing but Him.* He cherishes a life that isn't motivated and inspired by "service" or "results" alone, but is completely satisfied by His whisper and nearness, even in the midst of the mundane things in life. As well-known author and theologian C. S. Lewis simply but brilliantly stated, "God doesn't want something *from* us, He simply wants us." Dear reader, can I submit to you that God's ultimate desire is your heart?

The Church needs to have a whole new perspective of what God deems a worthy response to His indescribable sacrifice. In these days that we live in, to enjoy the gospel seems like a foreign concept. We are overcome with our desires to see results and frustrated by our failed attempts to accomplish giant feats for God. I am not against massive results or grand vision at all. However, it is imperative that such endeavors have their origin in and are sustained by the secret whisper of His presence.

I am not trying to stop believers from accomplishment; rather I just want to emphasize that anything that has significance to God must issue from Him, His presence, His voice. The true heart of the matter is the enjoyment of this glorious gospel: *The King of Glory offers His own blissful and empowering presence to men.* We must understand that such satisfaction is not merely a perk of God's presence in our lives, but rather the means by which He frees and empowers us to obey Him. *A Church that is not satisfied with God testifies to the world that God is not enough.*

Dear reader, we must reconsider our motives, our love, and our focus as Christians, for the crucial sum of all things is that He is a living individual to be continually experienced and interacted with; He must be the preeminent satisfaction and empowerment of our lives. If He is not, we run the risk of falling into that hollow counterfeit that deceives us into thinking we are more than we are. It will lead into empty, dry, cold, and lifeless religion. How many powerful, gifted, successful ministers do not walk with God intimately? How many professing Christians claim to live by the power of the Holy Spirit but have no real, interactive, fellowship with Him? And how many non-believers are chased away by a weak and joyless Church? How often is Christ presented as impossible laws rather than the gladness of our hearts?

Our inspiration is our past experiences with Him; our satisfaction must be our present experience with Him; our hunger is for our future experiences with Him. We must prefer touching Him over merely defining Him. We must prefer to move His heart more than to merely understand Him. He would rather us know Him than merely perform His works.

CHAPTER 18

Broken Bread for the Starving Soul

As the living Father sent Me, and I live because of the Father,
the one who eats Me, he also will live because of Me
(John 6:57 NASB).

In John 6:5 (NASB), we read that when Jesus saw the crowds were following Him, the first thing He said was, *"Where are we to buy bread so that these may eat?"* Shortly thereafter, He said, "Have the people sit down," and then *"He distributed to those who were seated"* (John 6:10-11 NASB 1995).

I want us to recognize that when we come to Jesus, His initial concern is for our nourishment. His first thought is, *I want to feed you.* But for Him to be able to satisfy us with Himself, He desires for us first to be seated. This speaks to us of rest and stillness. Just as the psalmist says, He makes us to *"lie down in green pastures. He leads* [us] *beside the still waters"* (Psalm 23:2 NKJV). The term *"still waters"* may be more literally translated as "waters of rest" or refreshment. God will not chase a man down to feed him. Only those who have come to Him in an attitude of rest will receive and eat. Do you recall Mary and Martha? God did not make Martha stop serving, but at the same time, He only gave His words to Mary.

Here in John 6:57, we see Jesus telling those who have come to Him and are hungry to sit down. This is an order, a command, if you will, that is tied together with His desire to feed them. He says, "Rest!" because He simply cannot and will not feed the person who will not rest—that one who refuses to relinquish all cares, activities, and efforts to wait upon the Lord in simple trust. That is why the Scriptures are clear to point out that He gave to those who were seated. We must obey this serious command from the Lord if we are to partake of the bread that both He Himself *is* and *gives*.

It is significant that Christ Himself gave the bread, which means that the bread issued out from His person and presence. The Old Testament calls the bread in the tabernacle, "the bread of the presence." Christ dispenses Himself as bread to those who will put their efforts aside and simply come to Him. Many people are pressing and working and fighting to get God to give them something of Himself, but it will not happen. We must recognize His desire to feed us, obey His command to rest, and then receive in His presence that supernatural bread from His own hand. Walter Buettler taught, "We don't get things from God by running but by sitting." Pastor and missionary Witness Lee is loved by some and hated by others; he points out something nonnegotiable in his book *The Tree of Life*:

> God's intention for man is not a matter of doing, but a matter of eating. If man eats well and eats rightly, then he will be right. God's intention is not that we serve Him, do good to please Him. God's intention is that we eat Him. He came that we may eat Him. He came to present Himself to us as life in the form of food. We have to take Him as food by feeding upon Him and eating Him. After receiving Him, the problem is not related to work, to service...but to eating. How do you eat, what do you eat and how much do you eat? God's intention is that man would simply take God Himself as his food. That man would feed on God.[27]

CHAPTER 19

Eating the Bread of Life

And Jesus said to them, "I am the bread of life. He who comes to Me shall never hunger, and he who believes in Me shall never thirst"

(John 6:35 NKJV).

Once I had short break at work and was looking for a place to eat my lunch. The only place I could find was at a long picnic table occupied by several young people with books. I shamelessly joined them at the table and quickly found out that they were culinary students studying and sharing recipes from their cookbooks. As I watched and listened, I perceived something: amid their pictures, conversations, opinions, and knowledge about food, not one of them actually had any food at all. In that moment, I saw a picture of the danger that is before the Church. Talk, study, books, materials, and knowledge don't mean we have the nourishment of Christ. We may have all the practices and yet be starving to death.

Memorized recipes and cookbooks cannot give sustenance. We memorize Scripture and cling to our Bibles with dogmatic belief, yet we stumble about malnourished and lifeless like the rest of the world. I have fallen into this trap more times than I would like to admit. If I found a man dying of hunger, I wouldn't be able to save him by giving him recipes or describing food to him. Even the greatest chef in the world will die if he doesn't eat food; he cannot draw an ounce of sustenance from his knowledge, experience, materials, books, or teachings. Men are dying in their marriages, suffering in their addictions, and wasting away from a lack of faith as they look to ink and paper alone for salvation (see John 5:39). Man's desperate need is Christ as nourishment. Man does not have the nutrition, health, or energy sufficient within himself to obey God unless he is satisfied by eating the Christ-manna. *Man is bound by his own lusts and self-centered cravings until he lies at the feet of Him who feeds with bread from another world.*

So here comes Jesus, who calls Himself the *"bread which came down from heaven"* (John 6:41 NKJV). He is the bread that *"came down"* and the bread that "comes down." He came down to the world and still comes down into our hearts by the Word and Spirit. There is a continual coming, or shall I say a perpetual reception, of the Son by the Spirit. We are alive in Him because we ate Him, but we also live our lives by eating Him.

John the Revelator called Jesus *"the Word of Life"* (1 John 1:1 NKJV). Our life source is His speaking, His voice. He is the living Speaking of God and our nourishment for a godly home, relationship, mouth, heart, employment, ministry, and life. Without His voice, we are empty and lifeless. David foreshadowed this dependency when he wrote, *"If You are silent to me, I will become like those who go down to the pit"* (Psalm 28:1 NASB). The digression of every Christian life starts at this point: malnourishment.

Ask yourself, "Do I hear Him in my life?" Let me illustrate the major difference between learning and hearing with this example. I used to prepare crab legs in the kitchen when I worked at the Pelican's Perch in Pensacola, Florida, but I couldn't tell you what one tastes like because I have never eaten one. You see, all the facts in the world about cooking crabs and all my outward contact with them in preparing them for others to eat never acquainted me with their taste. So it is with experiencing God; theologians around the globe have defined Him, but how many of them have eaten Him. *If we live merely learning and not eating, our heads become heavier than their hearts; our brains become full, but our hearts remain hollow.* We know, but we do not feel.

What is the answer for those people who have eaten Him at one time but are still living malnourished lives? The answer is a life of eating the Lord. In *Practical Lessons on the Experience of Life,* Witness Lee writes a paragraph on this very thing that is near perfection,

> The result of eating God is that we express Him. After we enjoy the divine life we express the divine life. God is life and His Word is also life. This Word speaks, unfolds, reveals and expresses God…for the Lord Jesus to say that He is edible means that God Himself is edible. Therefore, we can boldly declare that God is edible and that we can partake Him, eat Him and digest Him…. If we enjoy God as our nourishment, He will eventually become the constituent of our being. We must enjoy Christ as our life-supply.[28]

You may ask, "What does this mean? How can I eat Him? I read the Bible. I pray. I go to church. I sing songs and worship Him. But how do I eat Him?" Let me help you understand what transforms our cookbooks into a delectable buffet—the presence of God. The presence of God passes the Word throughout our brain and into our blood.

Jesus goes on to say:

> *Truly, truly, I say to you, unless you eat the flesh of the Son of Man and drink His blood, you have no life in yourselves. He who eats My flesh and drinks My blood has eternal life…. For My flesh is true food, and My blood is true drink. He who eats My flesh and drinks My blood abides in Me, and I in him* (John 6:53-56 NASB).

I apologize for suggesting something so elementary, but to eat something you must be in its presence. Is this too simple to point out? I really don't think so because it teaches us that the most fundamental aspect of receiving this spiritual nourishment is the sweet presence of God.

Without His presence, the letters in the Bible stay on the page, but in His presence, they are written in our hearts. In the presence of the Spirit, God becomes audible, tangible, visible, and yes, even edible to our hearts! If we do not have His presence, we cannot eat Him, and if we do not eat Him, we have no life in ourselves. These four words make a statement of the true state of our being without Him; we truly have *no life in ourselves.*

In verse 53, Jesus brought together two wonderful realities of the Christian life: eating Him and abiding in Him. *He who eats abides, and He who doesn't eat doesn't abide.* The way we abide in the divine life is by feasting upon Him.

I once asked my friend, Dr. Jeff Hubing, who is a New Testament scholar, about the tense of the phrase, "He who eats My flesh." His response was enlightening: "The better way to understand that phrase would be to say, 'the eating one.' We must realize that living and eating are as contingent upon each other in our spiritual lives as they are in our physical lives. That is the teaching of Jesus." As Witness Lee continues in *Practical Lessons on the Experience of Life,* "The Christian life is a life of daily experiencing the Christ we have received. The Christian life is a life of experiencing Jesus all the time."

Men constantly tell me, "You cannot live by experience." But my response will always be the same: "Without experience, we don't live."

God wants us to have a heavy, theological anchor during our intoxicating experience of the Spirit. Pastor and author Dane Ortlund likes to point out that reading glasses are not given to us to inspect but to look through. So, the Word is a means to the man. It is not an end in itself; it is to bring us into a deeper experience of God.

CHAPTER 20

Jesus, the Truth

Jesus said to him, "I am the way, the truth, and the life. No one comes to the Father except through Me"
(John 14:6 NKJV).

If I said, "Jesus is our salvation," I don't know of any professing Christian who would offer a rebuttal; as a matter of fact, most would nod their heads in complete agreement without fully understanding what this statement actually means. Salvation is generally understood as being saved from sin and eternal damnation through accepting Jesus' sacrificial or substitutionary death on the cross. Such an understanding, though correct, still falls miserably short of what that salvation means. *"Jesus is our salvation" means that we have been saved from a life apart from Him.* Let me explain further.

Jesus said, *"I am the...truth,"* because He knows that men will cling to truths but forget Him who is the Truth. History shows us that the human way is to separate God from our practice unto Him. We have a great blessing in the written Word, through which He has given us certain truths as guidelines for life in this world. But He never intended for us to learn them and practice them without His empowerment; He never intended for them to replace His presence. Rather, He wants to breathe and speak His very Self into us through the things written. He never intended them to lead us away from dependence upon Him.

I can't tell you how many times during street evangelism that I've come across that partier who knows a massive amount of Scripture or that homeless man who seems to quote a whole book of the Bible. These men only learned truths, but they do not know Him who is the Truth. They only have a mental image of Christianity; they neither hear Christ nor see Him because there has been no life exchange.

Jesus said the same to the Pharisees who staunchly advocated the words of God with all their might and yet were unable to see the Word of God right in front of their faces. Jesus said to them, *"You have neither heard His voice at any time, nor seen His form"* (John 5:37 NKJV). *Jesus teaches us through this that the spirit of religion is devotion to God without a living perception of Him.* Jesus was devoted to God through perceiving interaction with Him. *Religion is presence-less devotion.* It is morality without righteousness. It is information without revelation. It is knowledge without knowing.

Pilate asked Jesus the question, *"What is truth?"* (John 18:38 NKJV). I believe Jesus was completely silent before Him because if Pilate couldn't see the living Truth standing before him, no amount of lesser truths could help him. *We have lost Jesus as the Truth and have replaced Him with truths.* Because of this, men have judged their spirituality and nearness to God upon their knowledge of the Bible. Dear friends, the context of the Bible is only the means to bring us into a position of hearing His voice so that we may know Him. The words written must be written in us, and only His presence can perform such a wonder. It is true that God will not speak contrary to the Scriptures, but it is equally true that He speaks to us through the Scriptures in order for us to know Him who is the Truth. In the words of A.W. Tozer, "We have substituted logic for Life."[29]

CHAPTER 21

Jesus, the Life

Jesus said to him, "I am the way, the truth, and the life"
(John 14:6 NKJV).

Jesus said, *"I am the…life,"* because He knows that everything, no matter how religious or spiritual, is absolutely lifeless without His presence. He knows that people seek to live their lives for Him without drawing life from Him. I know that every single one of my failures was first the failure to let Christ be my life. The motto of the spirit of religion is this: "Give them everything but His presence." Why? Because *only His presence gives life.* This is why some hate religion while others die under it, because it only gives a picture of Jesus but never introduces the person of Jesus. Without the presence of Him who is life, there is only death.

Jesus laid down His life so that He might be our life; He gave His life to give life to those of us who give Him our lives, not just theologically, but in reality. Jesus is not just righteousness for us, He is righteousness through us. Many might deny this, but this is the way of the Spirit: being animated by Christ Himself. He must be our quickening life, our state of being.

We have been saved from the life that we received from our natural fathers. After the Fall, Adam reproduced after his own kind (see Genesis 5:3). Everyone lives from a defiled life source, defiled blood bent against God, bent toward self-preservation. Jesus came to rescue us from this selfish life by giving us His own life that is united with God's.

As Leonard Ravenhill said, "Jesus didn't come to make bad men good, but to make dead men live." *Our doom is that without the life of Christ, we do not possess life in ourselves.* The Puritans used to pray, "Grant me to feel my need of Your continual Saviourhood."[30] "He who has the Son has life; he who does not have the Son does not have life" (1 John 5:12 NKJV). Jesus is the Life, our divine animation, the righteous quickening of our being.

So if you have been looking for the Way, look no further, for you can find it in Jesus, in His presence and person. If you have been looking for the Truth, look no further, for it is Jesus, His presence and voice. If you are tired and worn out, lifeless and powerless, receive supernatural influence and strength from Jesus, for His presence and Word are the Life.

CHAPTER 22

Learning in His Light

For with You is the fountain of life; in Your light we see light
(Psalm 36:9 NKJV).

God Himself is with us through His words. Andrew Murray wrote, "In worship God takes us up to be with Him, and in prayer God swoops down to be with us." A few years back, I had a very vivid vision in prayer that will give a picture to that point. I was in a dark room, straining to read the Bible. It was fuzzy and very difficult to make out when, all of a sudden, a Light Being appeared a few feet away; and as I looked up at Him, He drew closer and closer. As He did, I was able to see clearer and clearer. Without His presence, I was blinded, but when I became aware of His presence and turned my attention to His person, He became like a lamp for me to see His words.

What am I trying to say? It is imperative that the Scriptures themselves be cracked open by the weight of His presence. Then His voice can come out of them and into us, and the transformation begins. For in His light, *"we see light."*

Once we come to the Lord and allow Him to be our satisfaction, which means we have given up on all other things and recognize that only He satisfies, this will inevitably produce in us an endless preoccupation with God Himself. David says, *"But his delight is in the law of the Lord, and in His law he meditates day and night"* (Psalm 1:2 NKJV).

This is a consuming, literal obsession with the person of God. We learn from this that meditation on God's Word brings an eruption of delight in God.

We must pray into the things God has shown us in the Scriptures. When we hold the Scriptures up to the light of God's presence in accordance with His directive, they suddenly come alive. When His sweet presence has opened my eyes to see the wonderful things in His Word, I feel as if the pages themselves are breathing. The more time we spend in His presence, the more we will love the Scriptures and become addicted to the electric thrill of God's voice that comes through them. The Scriptures are the straw through which the honey of Heaven flows. In this vein, I liken meditation to the suction by which we receive that honey. We cannot be in a rush during our daily reading of the Bible because haste always muffles our ears. Everything must be careful, deliberate, and important. Let us take our time and read the Scriptures differently from any other reading. We must desire more to hear than to merely learn.

CHAPTER 23

Interaction Opens the Scriptures

*And beginning at Moses and all the Prophets, He expounded
to them in all the Scriptures the things concerning Himself*
(Luke 24:27 NKJV).

There are countless theologians with a vast understanding of the Word
of God, yet their souls are severed from the God of the Word. You don't
have to be pure to understand what the Bible has recorded, but you
must be pure to see God (see Matthew 5:8). We must never forget that
amazing story of the disciples on the road to Emmaus. I believe that it
contains a valuable truth concerning our current subject.

I used to see Luke 24:27 as a self-evident truth that the Word of
God reveals Jesus. Though I do believe that the Scriptures do reveal
Jesus, there lies within that Scripture a higher truth. It is *the presence
of Jesus and interaction with Jesus that will reveal Jesus.* The Lamb is the
illumination (see Revelation 21:23). He unlocks the Scriptures to reveal
Himself; from glory to glory we see Jesus more and more.[31]

Let me explain it with this terrible analogy. I once had a cat. He
knew very well where his food was located, and he could bring himself
all the way to the can of "Seafood Delight" and push with his paw. I
can still see him propelling the container around the tile floor in the

bathroom. What I want to point out is that without my human superior intelligence and anatomy to aid him, he could only retain the knowledge of where his food was. That is similar to our case. No amount of knowledge concerning the location of food could ever bring any nourishment to our bodies. Without the Holy Spirit, the Bible is unable to open and give life. As Jesus noted in John 6:63 (NKJV), *"It is the Spirit who gives life."* Paul had the same understanding, stating, *"The letter kills, but the Spirit gives life"* (2 Corinthians 3:6 NKJV).

Though the moral wisdom of the Scriptures is in many ways practical and can be implemented in some fashion, I submit to you that, without the living presence of Jesus to quicken it, it will remain in the brain and never drop into our spirit and allow the person of the Spirit to perform His transforming work. Jesus did not die to make us merely students, but sons. This is what God is after. He is not into us seeking life by education alone, neither is it possible to educate ourselves onto the cross (see John 5:39). We must become something completely other than what we are. For this we need the work of the Spirit. This is the reason I believe many believers are stuck in the cycle of ever learning but never coming to the knowledge of the truth (see 2 Timothy 3:7). The whole of Christian maturity hinges upon knowing God, not simply knowing about God (see John 17:3). A. W. Tozer in his classic *The Pursuit of God* spiritually guides us:

> It is not mere words that nourish the soul, but God Himself, and unless and until the hearers find God in personal experience they are not the better for having heard the truth. The Bible is not an end in itself, but a means to bring men to an intimate and satisfying knowledge of God, that they may enter into Him, that they may delight in His Presence, may taste and know the inner sweetness of the very God Himself in the core and center of their hearts.

For this experience, we need a pure heart with a desire for Him alone. Scripture describes the heart as the spring from which flows all the streams of our lives (see Proverbs 4:23). Even our theology flows from our hearts. This is the reason why there is so much chaotic, crazy theology out there—if there is dirt in the fountain, there is mud in the streams. If there is dirt in the root, it brings forth bad fruit. Issues of the heart are the reasons why there are so many strange world paradigms. Yet if the heart loves, then God dwells within. Some people have studied themselves out of love. Leonard Ravenhill said, "We are not here to get to know the Word of God but to know the God of the Word."

CHAPTER 24

Knowing God's Goodness

But the anointing which you have received from Him abides in you, and you do not need that anyone teach you; but as the same anointing teaches you concerning all things, and is true, and is not a lie, and just as it has taught you, you will abide in Him

(1 John 2:27 NKJV).

Knowing God's goodness is not a matter of teaching, but of touch. Maybe I can say it this way: *Our Lord teaches by touch.* In 1 John 2:27, we are told that the *"anointing"* or in essence "the smearing" causes us to know. God's means of teaching us is touching us. He touches us to teach us of Himself. The things of God that He opens our eyes to in the Scriptures become ours, and we become them. Experience is nonnegotiable.

Do I love the Scriptures? Beyond question—they're a daily life source for me because they are the window through which I look upon the face of Jesus. Yet we can't study ourselves away from experience. The Bible is the blessed book of experience. We don't believe so that we understand. We believe that we may experience. This is the difference.

There's a story of a boy who found a beautiful flower. He adored the flower and showed everybody its beauty. He loved it very much. He then thought to himself, *I want to understand this flower.* So he began to open the flower, dissect it, pulling off petal after petal. He was thinking about it deeply and logically, pulling it apart until there was nothing left—no beauty left to adore.

And so it is with many people in their Christian lives. They begin lovingly adoring the Lord, and then they seek to explain and expound and understand, trying to apprehend God by logic. They pick God apart to the point that they have nothing left to adore. They study the beauty out of Jesus instead of worshipping the beauty of Jesus that the Scriptures reveal. I've seen this happen many times in my own life when I become lost in mental traps of human reason and hypothesis. But the light of faith demands that a man transcend the scope of his own reason, finally giving up and saying, "Oh, Lord, only You know." I tearfully say to you that I do not want to lose my love for Jesus in an attempt to define Jesus. I do not want to master theology at the cost of losing the sense of His presence. I want to keep my heart in love with Him. That is all. Look closely at these words from A. W. Tozer that he wrote in *The Pursuit of God:*

> God will not hold us responsible to understand the myster-ies of election, predestination, and the divine sovereignty. The best and safest way to deal with these truths is to raise our eyes to God and in deepest reverence say, "O Lord, Thou knowest." Those things belong to the deep and mysterious Profound of God's omniscience. Prying into them may make theologians, but it will never make saints.

CHAPTER 25

Clinging to Christ

My soul clings to You; Your right hand upholds me
(Psalm 63:8 NASB1995).

Oh, the clasping, the clinching, the gripping strain of the one who is inches from death. With all the energy and power that the human will can employ, a man clings to his saving element when his life is in jeopardy. Even among animal life, clinging is understood. Are you familiar with a cat's loathing of water? As if he would melt upon contact, he struggles to keep himself from it. It doesn't matter who tries to cast him into a body of water, he will sink his claws into the depths of that individual in a desperate attempt to remain apart from the water. As a matter of fact, a definition of the word *abide* is "the refusal to depart."

The cat seeks to abide, remain apart from the water, by refusing to depart from the individual. He becomes like living Velcro, attached to save his life. Can the picture of clinging be more vivid in the mind than the last effort of human self-preservation or the paranoia of a clawed creature? I say, yes, even more still, the unification of a branch with a tree—the oneness yet difference between the branch and the tree. The branch is the extension of the tree in which it abides, and the tree is the source of the branch that abides in it. *We abide by clinging, and we cling to abide.* The abiding life is the clinging life. The clinging life is the abiding life.

The actual Greek word Jesus uses for *abide* in John 15 is *meno,* and according to Strong's Concordance, its particular meaning is "to remain or abide." In reference to a place it means "to wait, or not to leave; to be held, kept continually; to continue to be present." In reference to time it means "to continue to be, to endure." In reference to a state or condition, it means "to not become another or different." The context is life in the Vine by the abiding branches.

CHAPTER 26

Jesus, the Only True Vine

I am the true vine

(John 15:1 NKJV).

The glorious Son of God informs us that He is the Vine. In John 15:1, Jesus used the first person personal pronoun, *I*, to refer to Himself. The fundamental truth concerning relationships is that a relationship is between two or more persons. It sounds elementary, but we must note that there is no relationship between a person and a building. Nor is there a relationship between a person and a system, or a person and a teaching, doctrine, or practice. A relationship is between two persons. Jesus said, "I," not things about Him, but Him, Himself. The subject at hand is the person, Jesus Christ; the real, currently living individual.

The striking revelation rings in our souls when Jesus says, "am." This reveals that abiding in the vine is a present happening. It has to do with right now. The fact that He is the vine is significant because He didn't say, "I will be the vine," or "I was the vine." Jesus said, *"I am the true vine."* In that moment in which He spoke, He was the vine. And because He is that vine, today as He lives, as sure as then, He is right now, *the* vine.

If Jesus is the true vine that implies that there exists a false vine or many other false vines. Jesus, in this very moment as your eyes cross these words, is the real, the genuine, the significant, the glorious vine (source of life), and everything outside Him is another vine. Whatever the vine or connection may be that is drawn in any person's life, no matter how positive it is or religious it seems, there is only one true vine; namely, Jesus Himself. The person, the living, existing, God-Man. It is imperative to note:

- Prayer is not the vine.
- The Bible is not the vine.
- The Church is not the vine.
- Pastors are not the vine.
- Ministries are not the vine.

What Jesus is saying by calling Himself the "true vine" is that everything else apart from Him is fictitious, counterfeit, imaginary, simulated, pretended, imperfect, defective, frail, or uncertain. The Son alone is life. At this very moment, the only real source of life is the person of Jesus Christ. You cannot draw from Christ at any other moment than the moment you are in. Right there where you sit, Jesus alone is the river of the divine life of God that can be and must be drawn from, now. Say this with me, "His presence is in the present." His leading is in this moment. Christ's image comes from Christ's presence and Christ's Word abiding in us and us in Him. *"Abide in Me, and I in you"* (John 15:4 NKJV).

CHAPTER 27

The Command to Remain Connected

...As a branch cannot bear fruit of itself unless it abides in the vine, neither can you unless you abide in Me. I am the vine, you are the branches. He who abides in Me, and I in him, bears much fruit; for without Me you can do nothing (John 15:4-5 NKJV).

Abide means remain, do not leave, continue to be present. David says in Psalm 16:8 (NKJV), *"I have set the Lord always before me...."* The soul can set the Lord before itself. And when Jesus chose to use the word *abide*, and David used the word *cling*, they carry an inevitable implication that it is not an impossibility to depart (see Psalm 63:8). It suggests that it is possible to not continue, to not be kept in Him. Abide is a command to remain connected, just as cling is a clinching to remain. The connection has a promised response: the sweet grace of the reception of empowering grace. We remain connected, and He flows inside. If the branch is connected to the vine, then it can receive the sap for life. Even the fruit in Galatians 5 is *"the fruit of the Spirit."* It is not ours. It belongs to His power and glory. We cling and sing. As A. B. Simpson, evangelist and founder of the Christian and Missionary Alliance, recognized after being filled with the Spirit, "I pray less and sing more."

Remaining connected is absolute dependence upon Him. The whole of the branch's resolve is to depend wholly upon the flow of life in the vine. As Andrew Murray so perfectly stated, "Remember the one condition; habitual, unceasing, absolute dependence upon Him."[32] Our command from the Lord is not to bear forth fruit or to yield our own increase, but rather to stay connected to Him who is the source of life, for the sap alone carries the nutrients and power for the branch's fruitfulness. The demand upon your life is nothing more than, "Cling to Me for life." Often, people want to be instantaneously delivered out of everything because they don't want to have to be dependent upon God every day. All that is happening to us is bringing us face to face with the truth of whether God is really enough for us.

Many ministers and Christians lack vitality in their lives or ministries simply because they are drawing their life from some defective, imperfect, or uncertain thing; namely, anything outside the living interaction with the person of Christ Himself. If the branch is not bearing fruit or producing signs of life, it is because its reception is not divine life. It is receiving something else as its source. Often, people are more connected with the ministry they are part of than the Lord Himself. In that time when something goes wrong or they find difficulty in the ministry, their whole relationship with Christ is jarred. Abiding in Him is something different. It is the *"in Me"* that brings about the *"in you"* and inevitably produces the *"much fruit."* The clinging life is the abiding life and the reproducing life. This is dependent not upon a practice or a minister or a ministry or a friend. It is dependent upon your real, interactive relationship with the person of Christ.

CHAPTER 28

Seeing Christ in All Things

Unto You I life up my eyes, O You who dwell in the heavens
(Psalm 123:1 NKJV).

Some people think that because we are busy, our attention to God will suffer in some way, but they fail to realize that the soul was made to do all things through staring at Jesus. The soul was made to perform all actions, no matter how mundane, unto the glory of God. This is possible in our lives, as children of God, only through an internal stillness and unbroken adoration of God that brings an infusion of life from the presence of the Spirit, which causes all acts to flow into the soul from God and flow out of the soul in excellence and thereby manifests the glory of God in everything. This is our individual participation in the Trinitarian fellowship through the blood of Jesus. He has rent the veil that separated man from the presence of God and merged the sacred and the secular (see Matthew 27:51).

The idolatry of placing my affections upon anything other than God will ultimately destroy me. As C. S. Lewis noted in *The Weight of Glory*, "Idols always break the hearts of their worshippers." But the utmost joys and pleasures are wrapped up in the setting of our affections upon Him. Once God has the affections of a man, He has that man. As Shakespeare wrote in *Hamlet* concerning the insanity of love, "How weary, stale, flat, and unprofitable seem to me all the things of this world." Love makes all other things seem worthless. When our hearts are set on God, only He holds supreme value.

The question quickly arises following the soul's deep satisfaction with the love of God: Can there be any pleasure without Him? Is it possible to exist any longer without His presence? Charles Spurgeon wrote, "Art thou the Bride of Christ and yet content to live without His presence?" David said, *"My soul* [affections] *clings to You"* (Psalm 63:8 NASB). Many times, a man's emotions begin to overtake his thoughts. Many times, the affections trump the mind. *When God has all our affection, He begins to swallow up our existence.* He actually consumes all the details of our lives because He has become life to us through gaining of all our heart's desire. We can say as the lovesick ones, "I cannot enjoy anything apart from Thee."

For instance, I recently took my children to the park, and as I observed the surroundings, my mind recalled a quote from Irish revolutionary Joseph Mary Plunkett. He wrote in his poem, "His cross is every tree.... His blood is every rose." As I turned all my affections toward Him, quickly every pavilion became a picture of the refuge of His person. Every rock became His written words. Every leaf became the healing of the nations. The shade became the cool of His presence. Every ray of the sun became the warmth of His love. Every refreshing breeze became the sweet wind of His Spirit. Every bird was His promise to care for me. Every sweet fragrance was the ointment of His name. Every grain of sand became His thoughts toward me. The lake became the still waters from the Shepherd's psalm. The sound of the children's lips became praise perfected, and His blood dripped from every rose. Even as I stared at the fish in the pond, I heard His whisper, *"I will make you fishers of men"* (Matthew 4:19 NKJV). My affections were overtaken with the insanity of love. As He woos our souls to Himself, our affectionate love for Him bursts out of our eyes in tears. I heard Leonard Ravenhill pray, "I pray…that we will have to pull the car to the side of the road because we cannot see through our tears."

CHAPTER 29

What Is a Saint?

Now, therefore, you are no longer strangers and foreigners, but fellow citizens with the saints and members of the household of God

(Ephesians 2:19 NKJV).

I recently heard a story of a young Catholic girl who loved to turn her attention every Sunday to the massive stained-glass windows of the saints in the cathedral during her Sunday school classes. The instructor one day submitted a question to the group of Catholic students. She asked, "Does anyone know what a saint is?" All the children began to look around at each other without a clue as to what a saint actually is. Then the little admirer of the stained-glass windows very simply stated, while staring right into a stained-glass icon of Saint Francis, "They are the ones that the sun shines through." Though the answer was so simple, even too simple, the simplicity of such an answer was the golden truth. It was the simple articulation and imagery of God's unification with humans; *we are those through whom the light of the Son of God shines.* There is nothing more humble than a life that continually looks upon Jesus Christ. Humility makes us transparent, and God shines through our individual color. God is light; and if we live in humility, the light of unobstructed fellowship with Him will shine through us to others in a sweet union of Spirit, fellowship, and life.

God, through Christ, has made us worthy by giving us Christ's imputed righteousness in order that we might be included in the fellowship shared by the Trinity. This is the glory of what Jesus has done for us, opening the veil completely so we may have full access. Paul told the Colossians of his gratitude for the gospel, *"Giving thanks to the Father, who has qualified us to share in the inheritance of the saints in Light. For He rescued us from the domain of darkness, and transferred us to the kingdom of His beloved Son"* (Colossians 1:12-13 NASB1995).

Christ is not only perfect, His work is as perfect as He is.[33] Most Christians believe that Jesus is perfect, but sometimes we think that His work, for some reason, needs to be improved upon. But as Jesus is perfect, His work is perfect. Paul is lifted by the colorful winds of the gospel into a rapturous worshipful appreciation in Colossians 2:13-15 (ESV), *"...having forgiven us all our trespasses, by canceling the record of debt that stood against us with its legal demands. This he set aside, nailing it to the cross. He disarmed the rulers and authorities and put them to open shame, by triumphing over them in him."*

We are free from the need to perfect ourselves for acceptance by God. Christ completely canceled the decrees against us. The wording for *"open shame"* or *"public spectacle"* in the New King James Version is the same as that which is used in ancient times when a king was conquered. The conquered king was stripped down and paraded through the town, humiliated. That is what Jesus did. He stripped the devil and paraded him through the streets by His own perfect work. He conquered him completely. If we believe this, we will find victory and liberty beyond anything we have ever experienced before such a conviction.

The only battle is a battle to continue to believe that Jesus has won the battle. Insufficient trust and faith in the gospel brings about an inability to experience the glorious freedoms that are given to us by Christ. All the freedom we need is in the gospel. Read these words written by Luke in the collection of the works of the apostles carefully. They are found in Acts 13:38-39 (NASB1995), *"Therefore let it be known to you, brethren, that through Him forgiveness of sins is proclaimed to you, and through Him, everyone who believes is freed from all things...."*

Who else has done these things for us? Who else can be these things for us? Christ's work is as matchless as He is. It is impossible for the Matchless One to perform any other kind of work than a matchless work. It is impossible for the Perfect One to perform any work that is not perfect. Perfect access is gifted to us. Complete deliverance is ours. It is time that we let this gospel work in us as it is in all the world, *"bearing fruit and increasing"* (Colossians 1:6 NASB).

We have the preeminence of Christ and the perfections of His work, and yet the gospel does not stop there. Paul says in Colossians 1:27 (NASB1995), *"To whom God willed to make known what is the riches of the glory of this mystery among the Gentiles, which is Christ in you, the hope of glory."* And most precious of all, we have His presence within us.

This is a summary of the perfect gospel: Jesus is preeminent above all. His work is as perfect as He is, and you have, by Christ's work, the installation of His presence within, that *"works in you both to will and to do for His good pleasure"* (Philippians 2:13 NKJV). Dear reader, Jesus loves you and is taken with you. He didn't just love you on the tree when He bled for you. He loves you right now. Revelation 1:5 (NASB) says, *"To Him who loves us."* The same demonstration of Christ's love on Calvary works in you right now. His loving work is finished, but it is currently finishing us. Herein is the whole of the devil's work: to block the sight of Jesus! (See 2 Corinthians 4:4.)

CHAPTER 30

Remember the Gospel

For I am not ashamed of the gospel of Jesus Christ, for it is the power of God to salvation for everyone who believes...
                                        (Romans 1:16 NKJV).

I programmed my Alexa device to respond to "Good morning" with, "Eric, remember the gospel. He is enough. Love Him. He alone is worthy." It is a daily reminder that He alone is God—Creator of Heaven and earth. He is all-knowing, all-powerful, yet He became a human being. He subjected His glorious, limitless person to the restrictions and frailties of a human body. His meekness and majesty cannot be compared to another. May He help us believe this, for in it we see His beauty.

I start nearly every morning remembering the preeminence of Jesus. I call to mind the Scriptures that declare, *"He is the image of the invisible God"* (Colossians 1:15). I call to remembrance the perfections of His work. He has freed me from all things by His blood. I turn my attention to His presence within. He has installed His Spirit inside me, and herein I link myself by the gospel to the living Christ, living inside me by His Spirit. I encourage you to do the same.

Take a look at Colossians 1:25-27 (NASB):

I was made a minister of this church according to the commission from God granted to me for your benefit, so that I might fully carry out the preaching of the word of God, that is, the mystery which had been hidden from the past ages and generations, but now has been revealed to His saints, to whom God willed to make known what the wealth of the glory of this mystery among the Gentiles is, the mystery that is Christ in you, the hope of glory.

This was Paul's stewardship. He preached internal Christ through the Spirit. Paul referred to this as *"the mystery."* To preach this mystery is to call the attention of the people to the riches of *"the hope* [expectation] *of glory,"* which is Jesus Christ experienced. *Our current experience of the Spirit is the foretaste of glory divine.* You can only be confident of glories to come by experiencing glory now. It is tasting the riches of Jesus that gives us confidence that we will feast upon Him forever. Prolific Christian writer John Owen wrote in *The Glory of Christ,* "If Christ is not Heaven for you now, He shall not be hereafter." And also, "If you do not enjoy looking upon Him now you will not enjoy seeing Him when He comes."

This is enjoying the riches of the divine life through fellowship with Christ, God's Treasure Chest. We gain access to the Divine Treasure Chest by laying our head upon His breast. Christ has an endless treasury in Himself and invites all, "Come, mankind, far and wide, and receive as much as you wish." We will run out of bags before His treasures are exhausted. *Christ is inexhaustible.* I encourage all to make their life's sole ambition to exhaust the inexhaustible riches of Jesus. The gospel is the open door to experience.

CHAPTER 31

Our Life Is in Our Looking

Looking unto Jesus, the author and finisher of our faith, who for the joy that was set before Him endured the cross, despising the shame, and has sat down at the right hand of the throne of God

(Hebrews 12:2 NKJV).

By faith His righteousness is imputed to us. By faith we are united with His death, burial, and resurrection. *"For you have died, and your life is hidden with Christ in God"* (Colossians 3:3 NASB). *That means God sees Jesus when He looks at you.* God is only pleased with Jesus. By faith, you stand before God as Christ, because Christ stood before God as you. We look to Christ and hide in His person. Outside of faith we are not clothed with Christ or hidden in Him. It is by faith we hide in Christ, and faith is exercised by looking up unto Jesus. Faith is the eyeball with which we look upon God. In the same way that we turned our eyes toward Him in the very beginning, we continue to turn to Him in absolute abandonment. That is living by faith.

It is by this wonderful faith that we are aware of the internal, sweet presence of God. *Faith is the setting our hearts upon the Lord.* A. W. Tozer wrote, "Jesus' power lay in His continuous look at God."[34] If our eyes are not lifted away from the earth, we will never see Him who is our help. *"I will lift up mine eyes...from whence cometh my help"* (Psalm 121:1 KJV). David wrote, *"To You, O Lord, I lift up my soul"* (Psalm 25:1 NKJV). And he also wrote, *"My soul waits in silence for God alone"* (Psalm 62:1 NASB). This is our being renewed daily: *"...though our outward man is perishing, yet the inward man is being renewed day by day"* (2 Corinthians 4:16 NKJV).

Compassion, patience, love, humility, and kindness are not necessarily things that you are, but things that Christ is when He lives inside you. You *"put on"* Christ's attributes by sinking into His wonderful rule, by turning attention to Him who sits at the right hand (see Colossians 3:12-14). Attention to the presence of Christ in our daily lives is what will accomplish love, patience, and excellence through us. We are not dependent upon ourselves; we are dependent upon Him through the empowerment of His presence. *The fruit of the Spirit are virtues that flow, from being connected to the Virtuous One.* When we touch Him who is full of virtue, His virtue comes into us. It has to first come into you before it can come out of you. When grounded in God, even in the day of distress, you will thrive. Andrew Murray said, "God longs to live your life for you."

For us to attain God's character, by God's infusion, I wish to specifically mention patience. The power of God is most perfectly seen in patience—in the patience of Christ, whose beard was plucked out. Enduring mocking, scourging, and spitting, He yielded Himself to nails, lashes, the spear, and even death. This is a patience that shows forth the perfections of Christ and is accessible to you by the power of God within you. Yet God does not merely grant us patience, but patience with joy. His heart is that we would be full of joy even during tribulations, trials, sorrows, and even death. You can be filled with joy that comes from another world. You can be filled with patience that is not of yourself or anything on this earth. This patience and this joy are impossible by man yet imparted by the Holy Spirit.

I read that Robert Murray M'Cheyne was asked, "Why do you always ask to be filled?" and he replied, "Because I leak." We have a continual need. When we are filled, we have no room for anything else. It also lifts all the dirt and debris out of the container. *There is not a way to walk worthy of the Lord apart from the filling of the Spirit.* Only the Spirit can do this, and as the Spirit fills you with His wisdom and understanding, it changes the way you think, it changes your value system, it changes the way you are on the inside, and that inside change causes an external change.

Your lifestyle is a witness. *God did not call us to do witnessing; He called us to be witnesses.* God never planned to win the world through witnessing; He planned to win the world through witnesses. It is something we become, having perceived and experienced the Lord. As we perceive and experience the Lord, we make the most of every opportunity to let Him minister through us.

We might ask, "What does it look like to walk worthy of the Lord?" Put simply, it is that you would please Him in every aspect of your life. This includes your marriage, your parenting, your workplace, your ministry, the way you are with your friends, the way that you speak, the way you conduct yourself, how you spend your time, and more. All these things are pleasing to God when our hearts yield to the rule of Christ. The genuine knowing of God produces these things in our lives. Knowing God is the issue, and I pray that you would come to know Him in a deep, transformative way. Your only strength is in the knowledge of God. As the Scripture says, *"Knowledge increases power"* (Proverbs 24:5 NASB).

Having our confidence in the blood of Jesus, we realize Colossians 3:12 (NASB), *"So, as those who have been chosen of God, holy and beloved...."* First, He has chosen us. Second, He has made us holy. Third, we realize we are loved. Take a moment and think upon this wonderful gospel. He chose you. You did not even know to choose Him. He separated you unto Himself from the decaying world, because He loves you with an everlasting love.

CHAPTER 32

Shining, Shimmering, Glorious Gospel

According to the glorious gospel of the blessed God which was committed to my trust

(1 Timothy 1:11 NKJV).

The first time I saw gold dust, I was at my mother-in-law's house in Atlanta. I had taken three days to fast and be alone with Jesus all day without any human contact until nighttime. On the second day, about twelve hours into it, I was lying on the bed and meditating on John 7:37 (NKJV), *"If anyone thirsts, let him come to Me and drink,"* and at four o'clock I got up off the bed to get my blood moving, and I saw gold dust splattered on the wall over the left side (my side) of the bed. I was staring at it for a long time, trying to figure out where it came from. Then it dawned on me that it was supernatural after it completely disappeared right there.

The experience was breathtaking; I needed to know why God did that. So after talking it through with a couple brothers and meditating on the possibility of its meaning, I knew. It meant that the message of my life was going to change to satisfaction with the glory of God through intimacy and rest. This message of satisfaction with His glory alone must go to the four corners of the earth. The bed represented intimacy or rest, gold represented glory, the text I was reading was satisfaction with Christ, and four o'clock meant the four corners of the earth. From that day on, all my desires shifted into this without any effort on my part. It is now the grace upon my life to speak of such a glorious facet of the Christian life—satisfaction with the glory of God through intimacy and rest in Jesus.

It is my deep conviction that the essence of the gospel is man's reconciliation with God; namely, the restoration of God and man finding pleasure in each other. What does this mean? It means that the relationship which was disrupted and lost through Adam's disobedience has been restored to mankind through faith in the finished substitutionary work of the one God-Man, Jesus Christ. Union between God and man experienced through interactive fellowship is the heart of the gospel. The good news is that He has brought us back into Himself to enjoy the sweet communion and harmony that He enjoys in His Trinitarian Self.

Dear reader, do you understand that the gospel means that we have been invited into the bliss of the Godhead? To live in, through, and by the sweet union experienced by God Himself? His love is unmatched. He has freely given Himself to us even though we have all rejected Him outright. He alone is worthy of all our hearts and lives. God's paramount desire is to bring men into Himself and place Himself into men. I cannot emphasize it enough: *The gospel is God offering His own presence to men.* To reject His presence is to reject the empowering, blissful satisfaction of His person from our lives.

What a gospel! We not only can recognize our depraved state without Him, but we can call on Him in response to the wonderful revelation of His love displayed on the cross. This wonderful gospel isn't just how we are made alive but is the means by which we live. Read it again: *We don't just live because of the gospel, we live by the gospel.*

CHAPTER 33

Son of God

For God so loved the world that He gave His only begotten Son, that whoever believes in Him should not perish but have everlasting life

(John 3:16 NKJV).

God acts in the unveiling of His Son. All of God's works are done by showing Jesus. Jesus is the beautiful redundancy of Christianity. We have one message. There is only one thing to say, and one thing to offer—Jesus! We have to get this inside us, recognize it, and believe it so we never stray into strange streams. Let us have a radical commitment to be reduced to only Jesus. I want people to be liberated by such a breed: the Jesus breed. Let us be a Jesus people who cannot stop proclaiming the lowly Son of God and Son of Man.

The fact that Jesus is called the one and the only means that nothing else exists in the mind of God. Consider Abraham and Isaac. God said to Abraham, *"Take now your son, your only son"* (Genesis 22:2 NKJV). Wait a minute. Abraham already had Ishmael at that point. Yet God referred to Isaac as Abraham's *"only son."* Why? Because to God, the only son who existed was the Son of promise. So it is with much of what is going on in the Church today. We cry this or that Christian-themed thing, and God says, "I have one Son. One thought. One desire. One happiness. One goal. One purpose. My Son."

If it's not in Him, to Him, and through Him, it doesn't exist in the eyes of God. That means your ministry exploits, ventures, and all. Even now, the timeless quote in a Charles Spurgeon sermon is crying out, "No Christ in your sermon, sir? Then go home, and never preach again until you have something worth preaching."[35] One will say, "Yeah, but Eric, we have all sorts of fruit popping up." Forget your fruit. He is the fruit. The only test is, *did it come from Him and go back to Him?* It's the only litmus test we have. He is the answer to all things. *"Come to Me,"* was not a mere religious idea, but the very prescription mankind needed for all of life (Matthew 11:28 NKJV). The "One Thing" is the only necessity for life (see Psalm 27:4).

CHAPTER 34

Christ the Lord

If you declare with your mouth, "Jesus is Lord," and if you believe in your heart that God raised him from the dead, you will be saved

(Romans 10:9 NIV).

We must understand that, if there were a way for Jesus to be Savior and not Lord, then "salvation" would never have dealt with the root issues in Eden (man's rebellion). The submission to the reign of Christ in the human soul is the teeth of the gospel; the lordship of Jesus demands the surrender to His rule. Jesus didn't come to give men forgiveness alone. Who doesn't want forgiveness? We could "save the world" just offering forgiveness, but He came to reconcile men to God. *Reconciliation is only a reality in submission to His rule.*

For the most part, churches in America have preached a partial gospel; because we are afraid to puncture people, we take the teeth out of the gospel. We must understand that to remove the necessity of our submission to His loving rule is to remove the good news from the good news. A lady said to me the other day, "God doesn't convict people to give their lives to Him in order to save them; He shows them His goodness, then they give their lives to Him." To which I replied, "Conviction is His goodness." He is so good to convict us. He is so good to take the management of our lives away from us.

The man who wants to manage his own life, knowing that God desires to manage it, is full of selfish ambition and pride, all of which must be laid at the feet of Christ. Because, without conviction there can be no repentance, and what is repentance if we maintain the ruling of our own lives? Our identification with Christ's cross is through surrendering our hands to be nailed with His.

Conviction is a gift straight from the good heart of God. The lack of delivering the fullness of the gospel brings men all the way to the door but refuses to tell them how to turn the handle. We cannot fall into the trap of preaching the power of the Kingdom of God without repentance, nor fall into the trap of preaching repentance without the power of the Kingdom. To be convicted is to be brought to the place where we can lay our lives down at the feet of Jesus. Without conviction, man only acknowledges Jesus. But to believe in response to an internal Spirit conviction is not partial or conditional. To surrender to this Kingdom is not withholding. Faith in its very essence of meaning is contrary to partiality. Paul explained in Galatians that any alteration by addition to the gospel will sever us from Christ. Pastor and evangelist David Wilkerson said in a sermon, "A diluted gospel is no gospel at all."

Jesus knows that He is worthy of our hearts and lives. He can demand all your love, for He knows that no one else can be to you what He can be to you. He is the only one who has the right to demand everything from you, for He is the only one who can totally satisfy you.

One of the most impacting statements on this subject is from Art Katz when he said, "The idolatrous religions are those that give men a small measure of religious satisfaction yet, they allow men to retain the lordship of their own lives."[36] It dawned on me one day that if the devil can seduce Christianity away from the cross, he will create one of the most successful "positive"—death traps that there has ever been. Paul warned about *"another Jesus,"* and a Jesus that isn't King, isn't Jesus (2 Corinthians 11:4 NKJV). A Jesus who doesn't remove you from being the manager of your own life is not King Jesus. *The greatest news in the world is that God will take your wicked-sinful-no-good management of your life and will resurrect it, giving you divine purity, power, and life.*

Death for life is the main principle of the Kingdom. The gospel is always death to the Giver and life to the receiver. Everything in God is gained by death. In *Experiencing the Depths of Jesus Christ*, Madame Guyon explained, "God gives us the cross, and then the cross gives us God." God has no obsession with death. He loves resurrection life! But the truth stands that *He can only resurrect what is dead*. Needless to say, any "gospel" that allows you to retain the lordship of your own life is no good news at all. It is not Jesus, but a manipulation of things through a message about "Jesus." It doesn't save because it fails to enter into the reality of what salvation is.

CHAPTER 35

Our Meek King

Behold, thy King cometh unto thee, meek
(Matthew 21:5 KJV).

Take note, the passage above did not say, "Behold, thy King cometh, powerful," nor did it say, "Behold, thy King cometh, wise." Is He wise? Of course. He is wisdom. Is He powerful? Absolutely. More than any other. Yet the passage emphasizes a very specific way that He comes: in meekness. *Meekness marks the arrival of Jesus.*

The one time Jesus opened His mouth to describe His own character, He chose the word *humble*. Jesus said, *"Take My yoke upon you and learn from Me, for I am gentle and humble"* (Matthew 11:29 NASB). If there is one thing that Jesus wants you to understand about what and who He is, it's that He is humble. He could have chosen any other word to describe Himself, yet He chose *humble*. See, He knew you and I, in the midst of His greatness, majesty, and splendor, would likely try to separate Him from His core internal reality, which is humility.

We are attracted to all kinds of God's externals. Yet when we are presented with God's internals, we often lose interest. Yet this very attribute is what houses the presence of God. Jesus was the tabernacle of God, was He not? He was the home of God on earth—the living, walking, manifestation of God's infinite glory. And He essentially says, if you're going to be a carrier of the glory, this is the characteristic that must be yours: humility. If we learn anything about Him, we must learn this: He is humble. We would rather hear Him say, "The carriers of the glory are disciplined and strong." However, humility is the character of Christ. One may see Jesus as this or that, yet He forever settles His character as humility.

CHAPTER 36

Attracting Grace

...He also predestined [us] to be conformed to the image of His Son...

(Romans 8:29 NKJV).

God wants us to look just like Jesus. If the Spirit works into us the nature of Jesus, then this is what submission to Him will produce. Jesus is humble. May His nature be ours. The New Covenant Scriptures go on to say, *"But He gives a greater grace. Therefore it says, 'God is opposed to the proud, but gives grace to the humble'"* (James 4:6 NASB).

Like a fountain from Heaven, grace is continually, perpetually poured into those who are humble. The opposite is true for those who lack humility: God resists them. In other words, He prohibits their entrance into His presence. In fact, the word *opposes* in the passage means to put your foot down to block the door from being opened. God literally blocks entrance to those who are full of pride. What is pride? Anything and everything that is not humble.

Pride is selfishness, self-glory, self-effort, self-exaltation, and self-consciousness. It's all about me, me, me, and more me. Christian preacher and author Vance Havner said, "If God came to save us, He came to save us from I, myself, and me. If He didn't come to save us from self-infatuation, I don't know what the Savior came to do." The greatest hindrance to everything that God wants to do in your life is your eyes fixed on you. In his song "Make My Life a Prayer to You," singer/songwriter

Keith Green sang it well, "It's so hard to see when my eyes are on me." *"The fear of the Lord is to hate evil; pride and arrogance and the evil way"* (Proverbs 8:13 NKJV).

James remedied this by saying, *"Humble yourselves in the presence of the Lord..."* (James 4:10 NASB). We see the Scriptures again link together humility and the presence of the Lord. They are connected, for God sews them together.

CHAPTER 37

Exalted into His Humility

And being found in appearance as a man, He humbled Himself and became obedient to the point of death, even the death of the cross

(Philippians 2:8 NKJV).

Did you know there is a difference between humility and humbling yourself? *Humility is Jesus' character. Humbling yourself is bringing everything low to His feet.* It's like this: When you humble yourself, the Lord will exalt you. Humbling yourself means bringing everything down to the feet of Jesus. Then from that place, God exalts you into the humility of Christ.

When He exalts you, He doesn't bring you out of humility. In fact, when He exalts you, He brings you up into the heights and glory of what true humility is. *Humility is the character and nature of Christ.* Humbling yourself is bowing low in honest bankruptcy before God, where you're able to lay in front of Him your very heart, motives, intentions, expectations, desires, family, possessions, calling, gifts, past, present, and future.

If Jesus sat physically in front of you right now and said, "We have to have a meeting about your heart," then the moment you made eye contact with Him, you would immediately see all the things in your heart that oppose Him. You would become overwhelmingly aware of everything that is not as pure as He is—impure motives, how you responded to a situation the other day, sin that's been hidden for a long time, and more. Yet He would look at you with love. And if you had any sense at all, you would look back at Him and say, "Here. Have it all. I'm broken, weak, and empty. I'm in dire need of You, Lord. Take my heart and my whole life."

If we go low before the Lord, He will rush in and fill us. Just as water seeks to fill the lowest place, the Holy Spirit will rush in to fill those who are low. Those who are low will be filled with God's presence. *This why so many are dry, because they are too high. When you go low, you find the riches of God's presence.* The reason why God raises up those who are bowed down is that those who are bowed down have renounced any desire to be raised up at all. They left it all at His feet.

CHAPTER 38

Servant-Hearted

... Yet I am among you as the One who serves
(Luke 22:27 NKJV).

This is our Christ whose humility is dually shown in what He put off (Heaven) and what He put on (humanity): lowly, meek, and humble. He could have always taught standing on the water. He chose not to because He is humble. As Andrew Murray said, "Jesus came to bring humility back into the earth."

"I am among you as the One who serves" (Luke 22:27 NKJV). Did you hear what Jesus said here? God who created all things and sustains all things by the power of His own words said, "I have come to you to serve you." What is a servant? One who puts the needs of another above his own. There's nothing like this in the universe. This is God's disposition.

People ask me, "How can I tell if I have the same servant-heart that Jesus had?" I'll tell you one good way: How do you react when someone treats you like a servant? This will be a good measuring stick to determine where our heart is. When someone is exalted above you, how do you react? If your desire is to lift up everyone above yourself, then you can only rejoice for those who are lifted up, because your goal is being accomplished! *You will only feel competition and comparison to the degree that you've placed yourself higher than others.* We must throw ourselves down at the feet of Jesus, for in humbling ourselves, we will find the riches of His character-producing presence.

Humility is the key fruit of the presence of God. The holiest of all was the humblest of all. We must have a fresh desire to be humble. Humility puts me where I am supposed to be and puts God where He is supposed to be. *Humbling yourself alone allows God to do everything for you.* You are still in control to the degree that you don't humble yourself. To the degree you don't humble yourself, you are still operating on a battery pack that's really low. Yet God is always maxed out and limited by nothing.

Andrew Murray said, "Humility is the displacement of self and the enthronement of God." Do you want God to rule your life? Humbling yourself at His feet is how He does this. Jesus is humility personified.

CHAPTER 39

The Good Shepherd

The Lord is my shepherd; I shall not want
(Psalm 23:1 NKJV).

There is a story/poem about a stray sheep who makes his way to another flock and its shepherd. When a couple of the sheep in the new flock see this stray sheep, lost and confused, hungry and tired, one turns to the other and says, "Do you see him there? I really want to know, why this confused sheep knows not where to go." The other sheep turns in reply, "It really must be that he has not a Shepherd such as cares for you and me."

Jesus, our tender Shepherd, is all we need to satisfy our souls. There is no need that the Good Shepherd cannot meet; all cravings are all filled in Him. *Sheep in the presence of the Shepherd are free from the need to want anything else.*

The divine leadership of the Lord leads beside still waters. It is important to note that only the Shepherd leads us there; we cannot access this point by ourselves. Jesus' call, *"Follow Me,"* implies we must stay behind His leading (Matthew 4:19; Mark 1:17; Luke 5:27; John 1:43 NKJV). Many of us want to head in front of Him and have Him follow us, but I remember hearing a preacher say, "Jesus did not die so that He may follow you." The Holy Spirit is not like Casper the friendly ghost who goes with you everywhere you go. *The Lord is with you everywhere He goes.*

These still waters are only accessed by divine guidance. He leads us to these waters both by His example before us and His presence with us. The Shepherd keeps His sheep near water. There is no need for any to suffer thirst along the way, for the journey is beside the waters. Dryness is a product of either taking a route that leads away from the Shepherd or failing to avail yourself of the abundant nourishment. What is the significance of the waters? The water is the quenching of your thirst and the washing of the Word. The fact that His leadership is in proximity to waters reveals to us that He leads us hand in hand into both His Word and His satisfaction.

Death's power is worthless next to the Shepherd's presence. Many would say that the *valley of the shadow of death* is a place of abandonment or spiritual dryness, but it is nothing of the sort, for the presence of the Lord carries and delivers us from all fear, even the fear of death itself (Psalm 23:4 NKJV).

When we follow Jesus as the Good Shepherd, the surrender of our own way means that we are even now the sheep of His pasture. As long as we remain sheep-like, we remain His. In being His, owned by Him, following Him, looking to Him, we can hear Him and recognize Him. It is the sheep-like heart that possesses open ears and allows the Shepherd to be everything.

CHAPTER 40

The Sheep of His Hand

Oh come, let us worship and bow down; let us kneel before the Lord our Maker. For He is our God, and we are the people of His pasture, and the sheep of His hand...

(Psalm 95:6-7 NKJV).

One person says, "I do not want to be a sheep. I want to be a warrior," or "A sheep? No, I wish to be an apostle." Dear friend, why do you wish to be something great? *As long as you are great, He cannot be.* Always remember that only one of you can wear the crown. Sheep do not look for leading; they look only to the one who leads. Much of our warrior mentalities are justifying human striving in the name of the Lord. We quickly become like self-dependent soldiers who believe they have enough knowledge and experience to accomplish the task themselves. As I heard one man say, "I no longer need to be led by the Spirit, because I know what He wants." This is pride. But the meek little lambs are simple and attentive to every movement of the Shepherd.

We cannot assume we have the right wisdom or are even able to retain the right heart to understand what He desires from us at any time. He is our only certainty. Sheep are free from burden and concern to make sure they are going the right way because they look at Him who is the Way. The sheep's simplicity is of such a kind they are reduced to simply looking at the Shepherd and remaining wherever He is. They know that, if they are where He is, they are safe. If His presence is your goal, you can never get away from His will because you would have to leave His presence to wander your own way.

"Why sheep?" you say. Sheep are much more interested in feeding than leading. Pure enough to realize that they do not know the way, they simply live in the nourishment of His presence. Content to be wherever the Sovereign Shepherd has paused them, placed them, or is moving them, they are certain His goodness will lay before them a quiet stream of refreshing, luscious green grass in a place safe from predators. For He is the good King and the Guide to whom must be given more confidence than we have in ourselves. You say, "Eric, I haven't been this way in my heart."

How good He is! Even if a sheep falls, it is unable to rise on its own. And He leaves the ninety-nine to find, rescue and return any sheep that has been distracted. He will joyfully pick it up and say through His smile, "Dear little lamb, you are always needing Me, and I am always here." Who could turn from such love? It is all that we are looking for.

A woman who tended sheep for nearly eleven years told me that, once the sheep fall on their backs and realize that they are unable to get up themselves, they quickly lose hope for life. They surrender to death; and though their hearts are beating and their lungs are breathing, they silently wait for death to claim them. They give up and feel there is no sense of going on. After she finds them on their backs, she picks them up and turns them over. But she cannot place them on their legs because they will not be able to stand. She will hold them until the blood returns to their legs, and they can then be placed back on the ground, totally restored.

How much are we like this. We fail in so many ways, soon discouragement sets in, and we feel we are useless. Every bit of hope seems to be gone, and we nearly surrender to despair. Then the Shepherd comes looking for us. Finding you on your back in brokenness, He swoops down to pick you up. He turns you right side up and then holds you close until His blood returns to restore your soul.

Sheep are helpless. Their helplessness is their safety, for it gives all responsibility to God. For in the words of Christian missionary to China Hudson Taylor, sheep are those "who are weak and feeble enough to lean on Him." Recognizing they have no power in themselves, at the feet of Jesus, they exchange their weakness for Him as strength. A. B. Simpson wrote that precious secret that I wish to whisper into your ear, "I found that it was Him coming in, instead of giving me what I need."

> I am Jesus' little lamb,
> Ever glad at heart I am;
> For my Shepherd gently guides me,
> Knows my need and well provides me,
> Loves me ev'ry day the same,
> Even calls me by my name.
> Day by day, at home, away,
> Jesus is my staff and stay.
> When I hunger, Jesus feeds me,
> Into pleasant pastures leads me;
> When I thirst, He bids me go
> Where the quiet waters flow.
> —Henrietta L. von Hayn, "I Am Jesus' Little Lamb,"
> The Lutheran Hymnal, 1941

Come all! Let us give ourselves to the highest privilege known to men and angels. *"Come, let us worship and bow down; let us kneel before the Lord our Maker. For He is our God, and we are the people of His pasture, and the sheep of His hand."*

CHAPTER 41

Eternal High Priest

Christ did not glorify Himself to become High Priest, but it was He who said to Him: "You are My Son, today I have begotten You." As He also says in another place: "You are a priest forever…"

(Hebrews 5:5-6 NKJV).

The root word for the priest is *pillar* because pillars touch the earth and go to the heavens. Jesus is our High Priest or Pillar because He simultaneously touches the heavens and the earth. *"…He lifted them and carried them all the days of old"* (Isaiah 63:9 ESV).

I wish to carve into your heart today this convicting truth: *Pleading for others comes from seeing God.* Do you recall Moses' intercession for God's rebellious people in Exodus 32 occurring after his encounter with God on the mountain? Think back upon Abraham's intercession for Lot in Genesis 18; did it not follow his encounter with the Lord?

Shallow prayer lives know nothing of pain in the hearts of others. When we see Jesus, and we draw near to His heart and begin to feel His heartbeat, we know that He is praying on our behalf. If you have never felt this pain for others, it is okay, but we must realize that it is something God desires to share with us. Let us open our hearts to God and pray, "Lord, take me into such a private union with You that I might hear Your high priestly prayers and give them sound before God within the sole witness of my walls."

CHAPTER 42

Among the Golden Lampstands

John, to the seven churches which are in Asia: Grace to you and peace from Him...

(Revelation 1:4 NKJV).

We must not forget that John was a Jew. Knowing well the most famous blessing in the Torah, He was moved to start his letter by hinting at the Aaronic-priestly blessing in Numbers 6—that Jesus' face, His grace, would shine upon us and give us peace from Him who is, who was, and who is to come. John was revealing to us that the final Priest had come. The final blessing had been made. The fulfillment of the shadow is in the words that follow, which is the unveiling of the person, Jesus Christ, *"And in the middle of the lampstands I saw one like a son of man, clothed in a robe reaching to the feet"* (Revelation 1:13 NASB).

John wrote a description with ancient prophetic roots. This description of Jesus connects us with Exodus 28, in which the priests wore robes that extended to their feet. From the start of this Epistle, we see Jesus is the Son of Man who will rule over everything, wearing a priestly garment, which refers to His perpetual, unending, everlasting priesthood—standing before God on behalf of all people. Hallelujah!

Revelation 1:15 (NASB) says, *"His feet were like burnished bronze, when it has been made to glow in a furnace."* Because His feet are visible, we know that Jesus is not wearing shoes here. This is symbolic of the priests, who also did not wear shoes in their service. When Moses encountered God at the burning bush, he was instructed to take off his shoes (see Exodus 3:5). God was communicating to Moses that Moses would be the one to stand before Him and the people. Even as Moses was faithful over God's house, Christ was even more faithful over His (see Hebrews 3:2). The bronze speaks to testing and refining. Jesus walked on this earth, in this life, in our midst, as the Man-Priest, passing through all the testing necessary, on our behalf.

And then in Revelation 2:1 (NASB), Jesus is *the One who holds the seven stars in His right hand, the One who walks among the seven golden lampstands.* The seven stars in Christ's right hand represent all spiritual activity under His domain. Yet the second part of this passage is incredible. He *walks among the seven golden lampstands.* The priests of old walked among the lampstands and trimmed the wicks. They were the keepers of the flame. Jesus was revealing Himself to those who have lost their flame of love as the One who will keep the flame. If they will turn their attention back to Him who is the Keeper of the flame, then He can come in and keep the flame of first love.

Christ's message to Ephesus is the first of the seven letters to His seven churches, and the issue is first love—reminding us of His priority in our lives. He could have talked to Philadelphia or Laodicea first. Yet He got right to the primary matter. "First things first, love Me." I can hear His tender whisper, "Let Me tend to you. Let me keep you. If you go on without Me, I cannot tend to you. If you do things for Me without coming to Me, I cannot tend to you."

How precious is Christ our Beloved High Priest? Let Him show you where you have left Him. Let Him show you where you have replaced Him. Turn all your heart over to Him, and He will do the rest.

CHAPTER 43

The High Priestly Prayer

I ask on their behalf...

(John 17:9 NASB 1995).

Dear reader, becoming numb toward truths we have heard more than once is a common human problem. I urge you now to shake yourself awake and realize the immensity of John 17. In it, you're hearing Jesus pray. He prayed not some far off, ancient prayer for an Israel past, but for you who are reading these very words. This collection of words gives you a glimpse into the desires of Jesus for your life. These words are breathed by Christ for you. This is not a mere mortal praying from the mind of a man, but the One in whom *"all the fullness* [of the Godhead in bodily form] *should dwell"* (Colossians 1:19 NKJV). His perfection gives an eternal potency and perpetual power to His intercessory request. His lips drip gold into the timeline of history, shaping the future of all those who believe. Though His pleading was uttered many years ago, its force carries us through this very day.

John 17 is commonly known as Jesus' High Priestly Prayer. The reason this holy utterance is called such is because of its mediatorial nature, which means, Jesus our "Great High Priest" is standing between us and God praying. Spurgeon has clearly explained the mystery of Christ's perfect priesthood in a statement as lively as molten lava, "We stand before God as Christ because Christ stood before God as us." And we may add, *we are able to live a life of coming before God because Christ stands before God for us.* Pastor and abolitionist E. M. Bounds' famous quote aptly defines such a "high priestly" ministry, "It is a great honor to stand before men on behalf of God but an even greater honor to stand before God on behalf of men."

CHAPTER 44

Up with Our Hearts

Jesus spoke these words, lifted up His eyes to heaven, and said...
(John 17:1 NKJV).

After He spoke from God to the disciples in John 14-16, Jesus turned and spoke to God *for* them. Here we learn from the Holy Rabbi that we must pray for those to whom we preach. The link between teaching and prayer is one breath. As soon as His sermon ended at the close of John 16, we see in the first verse of John 17 (ESV) a phrase noting continuation, *"When Jesus had spoken these words...."* He then began the High Priestly Prayer.

"He lifted up His eyes to heaven," the unbroken sequence forever links the unique spiritual teaching to this rare earthly prayer. Famed Greek New Testament scholar A. T. Robertson wrote concerning Christ lifting His eyes to Heaven, this is "Christ's usual way of beginning His prayers." It is the psalmist-like disposition; looking up toward God.[37] In the ancient call to prayer "Sursum Corda"—"up with your hearts"—I see great significance in the fact that Jesus first looked at the Father before He turned to pray for others. This follows the pattern that He taught the disciples in Matthew 6:5.[38] *"When you pray,"* Jesus said, you are to first look directly at the Father, *"say, Father"* (Luke 11:2 ESV). This must have first place before we ever begin to intercede for God's purposes, *"Your kingdom come, your will be done, on earth as it is in heaven"* (Matthew 6:10 ESV).[39] *No matter how important God's purposes are, they*

will never be more important than God Himself. The Father must take precedence over guidance or personal need: *"Give us this day our daily bread,"* and, *"lead us not into temptation"* (Matthew 6:11,13 ESV). Jesus knows this. Jesus taught this. Jesus' heart is fixed in this exact divine order; Father first. We must live in this internal Christlike arrangement. In the concluding prayer of Jesus' life, Jesus lifted His heart to God, and the disciples were lifted with Him.[40]

Jesus seemed to have three things on His heart: His Father in John 17:1-5, His apostles in John 9-19, and all subsequent believers in John 17:20-24. His fixation upon His Father was very precise, *"Glorify Your Son that Your Son may glorify You"* (John 17:1 NKJV). This glorifying of His Son is the very root from which springs all the things for which He prays. This teaches us that there exist no other grounds upon which any intercession can be made. The Father and His glory must be our only impulse. Such a motive will remove vain-glory and selfish ambition, the most common sabotage of the prayers of men (see James 4:2-3).

Christ being raised from the dead and ascending into glory is the crux of the unified glorification of the Father in the Son, returning to the glory He shared with the Father before the foundation of the world. Read this next part carefully. By the means of this glorification, He would be enabled to send the Spirit so that eternal life might be given to all the Father had given Him.

Jesus pointed to His resurrection as the means by which He can impart the glorious life-supply of the Spirit into men with the unfathomable goal of men and God being made one. One by life. Inclusion into His family. Shared union with the Father by Him. It is interesting to note that Jesus began the High Priestly Prayer with that unique pull upon the heart of God, *"Father."*

CHAPTER 45

Communion Is the Covering

...Holy Father, keep through Your name those whom You have given Me...

(John 17:11 NKJV).

Jesus continued His prayer, standing on His established platform of knowing God. He requested that the Father keep, through His name, those who were given to Him. What does it mean to be kept through His name? The name of the Lord is the reality of His person. John Wesley, evangelist and revival leader wrote, the Lord's name is "all Thy attributes and paternal relation to believers."[41] Dr. Craig Keener wrote, "Moses announced the name of God (Exodus 3:13-15). More importantly, when God revealed His name, He revealed His character and attributes (Exodus 33:19,34:5-14)."[42] *To be kept in the name of the Lord is to be kept in union with Him.* This is not a union by way of a character and way of living chiseled out by the arm of men, but rather the sharing of His own Spirit and glory which reproduces His own character and attributes.[43] It's just as Paul linked the glory (of the Spirit of the Lord) beheld with transformation into the same image (see 2 Corinthians 3:18).

Jesus is not just looking for people to fall in line by way of obedience. He is looking for sharers in His glorious life. *Obedience is only the proof of love because obedience is the fruit of love.* Obedience is not a calculation in which one says, "If I do this, this, and this, then I get that." It's not a means of obtaining a result. If we do this, we separate obedience from the person. Forget obedience that's not connected to the Man, Christ Jesus. Be in love with Jesus and He will work in you to obey Him, and that's the only kind of obedience that He will accept. *Obedience is when a man's heart is yielded to the extent that God can perform through the man the things He has spoken to the man.* Even if we could obey God on our own, it wouldn't please Him. He is pleased with Christ and Christ alone. Jesus, knowing this, draws men into Himself by way of installing His life into men.

As Jesus prayed for the disciples to be preserved, their protection was in the same breath as their union with God in Christ. John Wesley with the precision of a fine poet wrote, "The Christian is kept from evil by greater attractions to Christ." I submit to you that *union is expressed in communion, and communion is presented to us as our covering.*

If we knew Christ's intercessory prayer for us, we would never fear. Imagine the Lord taking you into a vision and you see Jesus on His knees before the Father, praying by name for you. Can you see the Melchizedek-Christ standing before God with your name glowing on His chest? My friend David Popovici, one of the greatest men of God that I know who is currently giving his life to preach the gospel in hostile areas, told me he was once yearning, "Jesus, Jesus, Jesus!" and in that moment, the Lord showed him Jesus looking at the Father, saying, "David, David, David!" Their cries met. The glory of intercession is when the tears of Jesus come out of your eyes, when you give voice, in the earth, to the Voice before God in Heaven. How beautiful is our Heavenly Priest! Matthew Henry's Commentary statement is a perfect closure, "Let me have this, and I desire no more...to take the comfort of His intercession; and though this prayer ended, 'He ever liveth to pray for us.'"[44]

CHAPTER 46

Do You Want to Know the Secret?

But you, when you pray, go into your room, and when you have shut your door, pray to your Father who is in the secret place; and your Father who sees in secret will reward you openly
(Matthew 6:6 NKJV).

Recently, I had a dream. A very special person whom I highly respect as a man of God came to me in the dream and said, "Hey, do you want to know the secret of union with God?"

I said, "Yeah, I do."

Then he grabbed me and pulled me into a room away from everybody else. He shut the door. I leaned in to hear the amazing words of wisdom that would reveal to me the secret.

He then simply opened his mouth and softly and intimately sang, "Jesus, I love You. Jesus, I love You. Jesus, I love You." He completely forgot about me. He even forgot about himself. He continued, "Jesus, I love You."

When I woke from the dream, I thought to myself, *You know, he never told me the special secret.* Then I realized he was exemplifying the secret for me. It was this:

1. Get away from people.
2. Shut the door.
3. Forget yourself.
4. Forget everyone else.
5. Lift your heart in tender love to Christ.

That's the secret. It is tragic to admit, but I feel that, sometimes, we want something more than that. Yet there just isn't anything more than to love Him, because *in loving Him, we receive Him*. He is everything. The eternal object of love.

CHAPTER 47

Abraham, a Friend of God

And the Scripture was fulfilled which says, "And Abraham believed God, and it was credited to him as righteousness," and he was called a friend of God

(James 2:23 NASB).

It is an undeniable fact that God favored Abraham, for from the loins of Abraham's faith, God set aside a people for Himself. The chosen people of God go back to this one man's personal relationship with God. Known as the "father of faith" and the "friend of God," Abraham shared a unique and historic relationship with God.

Today, many love that label, "friend of God," and I know that through faith in the perfect work of the cross and the gift of the Spirit, we are all made God's very own family. But there is something that we cannot overlook about this special relationship that God shared with Abraham. I believe in Genesis 18 the Lord revealed a progressive picture of Abraham's intimacy with God that we can tap into. Through the Spirit, I wish to unfold some amazing truths about sinking deep into the ocean of knowing God and being united with His purpose and heart.

In Exodus 3:6, God identified Himself as *"the God of Abraham."* Though Abraham was not perfect, God's deep relationship with him reveals the fact that He chooses to identify Himself with flawed people, simply because they believe, love, and obey Him. It is evident that Abraham's fellowship with God brought him to an incredibly intimate bond with God—he is the only man singled out in his day. This mutually affectionate relationship was a bond of covenant friends. Think of how deep this bond went, where God questioned whether He should keep a secret from Abraham. Did you catch that? God actually thought to Himself, *"Shall I hide from Abraham what I am doing?"* (Genesis 18:17 NKJV). God didn't share with Abraham what was coming just because He could, but because He desired to.

God's communion with Abraham was at such an intimate place that God unfolded His own future plans in no uncertain terms; Abraham was told exactly what God was going to do—where, when, why, and how. And here is the most amazing part—this information was an invitation to intercede, an opportunity to co-labor with God.

Many of us love to think that our own relationship with God is at this level of intimacy, but so few of us have ever been divinely shown specific future events and invited to pray through them. Do you know God like this? Is this intimacy a reality in your life? Does God desire to open His blueprints before your eyes, giving you specific details to carry out? I am not just referring to unveiling the mysteries revealed in the Scriptures concerning His plan for the ages, but also His present work in your own family, friends, church, city, and nation. This, my friend, is the definition of a covenant friend of God: someone who has God's trust. *Trusting in the Lord begins this relationship; your trust in God should lead you into faithfulness to God where He can trust you.*

CHAPTER 48

From Servants to Friends

No longer do I call you servants, for a servant does not know what his master is doing; but I have called you friends, for all things that I heard from My Father I have made known to you (John 15:15 NKJV).

Jesus basically said to the disciples, "I call you friends." These are those whom He knew had already left everything to follow Him and would eventually give their lives in faithfulness to Him. Just like Abraham, they were those with whom the Lord found it desirable and necessary to share His specifics. Can you imagine God saying to Himself, "Shall I hide from [insert your name] what I am going to do?"

For example, perhaps a family member of yours has rebelled against God and is partying with other nonbelievers, and while you commune with God, He shares with you that the whole party is going to go up in smoke. When you recognize that information as an invitation to intercede, you begin to pray for mercy and salvation for your loved one. Later, you find out that a disaster did occur at the party, but a good Christian friend who felt uneasy about being there took your relative away just before the catastrophe.

God does many things on earth this way, inviting us to take part in bringing the Kingdom of Heaven to earth. This is why He cherishes His friends: simply because they listen to Him, because they commune with Him, and because He can trust them. Doesn't this kind of relationship sound desirable to you?

Maybe you already live in this place. Praise God! But, I submit to you that there is always more in His heart for those who are willing to plunge into it. If you haven't experienced this, do you want to? If you have, do you want more? How do we reach this place of friendship and trust?

CHAPTER 49

Dwelling in His Shadow

Now the Lord appeared to Abraham by the oaks of Mamre,
while he was sitting at the tent door in the heat of the day
(Genesis 18:1 NASB).

The Lord appeared to Abraham *"while he was sitting."* Abraham was not running, standing, leaning, or even sleeping. Abraham was sitting, consciously resting, still and alone. Don't let this slip by unnoticed.

Where exactly was he sitting? *"At the tent door."* What is the significance of the tent? Well, do you recall that Abraham had been called out from his home to enter a land that he did not know? He had torn his heart from his homeland and family to obey the voice of God (see Genesis 12:1-3). His life is the testimony and model of our earthly sojourning as aliens and strangers in this earth (see 1 Peter 2:11).

The tent is a statement, declaring that this world was not Abraham's home and that, despite an earthly Promised Land, he waited for something from Heaven (see Hebrews 11:10, 14-16). Abraham refused to sink his feet into the soil of this earth simply because of the word that the Lord had spoken to him.

Under this tent, Abraham was resting in the shade from *"the heat of the day."* What a wonderful picture: Abraham rested under the shadow.

Doesn't that same picture find its home in the lover of Song of Solomon 2:3 (NKJV)—*"I sat down in his shade with great delight"*—or the psalmist in Psalm 63:7 (NKJV), *"In the shadow of Your wings I will rejoice"*? Abraham was resting, quiet, and delighting in the shade of the Most High.

Friend, this is where the encounter realm is found—resting in His sweetness and hiding beneath His great love that obstructs the inevitable heat of life. Before we can understand why Abraham's friendship with God brought him into contact with the heart of God, we must understand the spiritual life that Abraham lived with God: Abraham rested under the shadow of the Almighty; he dwelt in this place of shade; he stayed in the refuge of God. The ground for life-defining encounters with God's glory is the daily experience of His glorious shadow.

CHAPTER 50

Opening the Eyes by Adoration

Unto You I lift up my eyes, O You who dwell in the heavens
(Psalm 123:1 NKJV).

In the midst of the heat of life, under the shadow at the door of his tent, Abraham *"lifted up his eyes."* The lifting of the eyes to the Lord is a picture of worship because we choose to fix our attention above the earthly cares of life and ascend to God, moving beyond the horizontal plane into the vertical. Abraham was able to look unto God without hesitation and reservation because he had already left everything for Him.

This faithful old man, having already proved God's faithfulness, neither strived nor strained, but simply looked up from his place of rest in the shade. Here, in adoration, he saw. Friend, this is also where you will see; *as you adore Jesus, you will see Him.*

Abraham lifted his eyes above the world unto God and looked with his eyes, giving his attention to God's presence. And he saw three persons. Though two of these were angels, it is interesting to note that three appeared to him. How utterly perfect this symbolism is: The vision is a triune vision. The vision of God is always threefold, revealing the Father by the Son and the Son through the Spirit.

CHAPTER 50

Opening the Eyes by Adoration

CHAPTER 51

Being God's Resting Place

My Lord, if I have now found favor in Your sight, do not pass on by Your servant. Please let a little water be brought, and wash your feet, and rest yourselves under the tree
(Genesis 18:3-4 NKJV).

It is wonderful to note that these three persons stand opposite Abraham. The vision of God is always completely opposite to what we are. Every time we truly see Him, we should be utterly convicted of how much we are not like Him, for He is holy and altogether separate from all things. He is other than us at every point, and our vision of Him will always reveal the same.

Abraham had a vision of three persons opposite to where he was, and his vision of them infused him with a great need to run to them. Gripped with desire, Abraham must respond. For us, all God has to do is reveal Himself, and the magnetic attraction of His nature and person causes us to leave everything else behind. (I can hear the Lover sing, "Draw Me and I will run after you.") Running to Him is a lover's action.

Notice that Abraham didn't run up to the visitors and start shaking their hands as if he were like them, but he threw himself to the ground in worship (see Genesis 18:2). *Worship always produces worship.*

Adoration always plunges you deeper into adoration. Abraham was humbled in adoration, low at the feet of these three.

I asked my friend Andrew Lamb, pastor of Acts 2 Church in Orlando, Florida, "If Jesus were to show up in your room one morning in prayer, what would you say to Him?"

His response was amazing: "Don't leave!"

Abraham said something similar: *"My Lord, if I have now found favor in Your sight, do not pass on by Your servant"* (Genesis 18:3 NKJV). God had come to visit him, and Abraham begged Him to stay.

Notice that Abraham addressed God as *Lord*. The kind of individual who has rich communion experiences with God is the one who submits to God as Lord. In Luke 6:46 (NKJV), Jesus says, *"Why do you call Me 'Lord, Lord,' and not do the things which I say?"* Today, many profess God as their Lord because they know that is what He is supposed to be, but they refuse to submit to Him. Abraham was not this way. He acknowledged God as his Lord because he had already left everything in response to hearing God's voice.

Abraham also called himself *the Lord's servant*. A servant is someone who lives to meet the needs of another. Abraham lived to meet God's needs; he had left all. He lifted up his eyes, he looked to see God, he lay before the Lord, and he immediately longed to serve Him and sought to be God's resting place: "Please let me wash Your feet. Please rest under the tree" (see Genesis 18:3). I wonder if this wasn't what Jesus referenced when He said that the Father, the Son, and the Spirit would make their abode in us? *"Jesus answered and said to him, 'If anyone loves Me, he will keep My word; and My Father will love him, and We will come to him and make Our home with him'"* (John 14:23 NKJV).

After they ate together, God spoke first to Abraham about Abraham. He looked into Abraham's heart and reminded Abraham of the deep purpose that had been directly placed in Abraham, the promise He Himself had given (see Genesis 17:2). And though God's word to him would still be tested, God spoke encouragement and affirmation deep into Abraham's being (see Genesis 22). *In communion, the first thing that God addresses is our own hearts.*

CHAPTER 52

"Shall I Hide from Abraham?"

The friendship of the Lord is for those who fear him, and he makes known to them his covenant

(Psalm 25:14 ESV).

After dealing with Abraham's deepest, most vulnerable parts, God made this statement: *"Shall I hide from Abraham what I am doing?"* (Genesis 18:17 NKJV). Except for Christ's prayer in John 17 or Moses' intercession for the Israelites, this statement sets in motion perhaps the most incredible conversation recorded in the Bible that God has with a human on behalf of humanity. It is important to note that both Christ and Moses deeply encountered God before their intercessions as well. I have said it before and will say it again: *Intercession is by invitation only.* Man does not just come up with his own plan of salvation and then manipulate God into it by kicking and screaming. Intercession is a product of laying your head upon His breast; it is hearing the vibration of God's beating heart.

Dear reader, God has called you to this very same place. He longs to be desired and seeks to be sought. Do you live in a tent as a sojourner and stranger in the earth, or have you sunk your feet so deeply into the soil of this earth that you cannot move when He calls you? Only from the stranger's tent can one truly rest in the shade from the heat of the surrounding desert.

Even if you live detached from this filthy age, are you resting in the shade, or are you moving and striving to make things happen? *Only from a place of rest can a man lift his eyes and look up to God.* As we wait upon Him, and focus our attention on Him in adoration, He will manifest Himself and reveal the triunity of the Godhead. And just like Abraham, you will know His holiness and run to Him that you might cast yourself at His feet, looking to serve and worship your Lord and God.

He will sup with you under the tree and encourage you with His own speaking. He will include you in His plans because you are His friend, and He desires to invite you to share His heart in intercession.

CHAPTER 53

Naked Trust—Letting God Be "Only"

For who in the skies is comparable to the Lord? Who among the sons of the mighty is like the Lord, a God greatly feared in the council of the holy ones, and awesome above all those who are around Him? O Lord God of hosts, who is like You, O mighty Lord? Your faithfulness also surrounds You
(Psalm 89:6-8 NASB1995).

I graduated from the Brownsville Revival School of Ministry in 2001. In 2003, I started working at Christ for all Nations (CfaN), the ministry of Reinhard Bonnke. I was laid off at CfaN in 2007 and started working construction until God spoke deeply into my being in the summer of 2010. He said, "I want you to be My spokesman." After a two weeks' notice, I quit working construction and started giving my life to the gospel alone.

Since that day, God has been gracious to back His gospel with signs, wonders, and miracles. Since my wife, Brooke, and I founded Sonship International, hundreds have surrendered their lives to Jesus in response to the gospel. The heart of Sonship International's mission is to bring the Church into a deeper experience of God in their daily lives. We are fueling the revolution of the Jesus people—seeking oneness with God through surrender, and teaching on the inner life and the interior matters concerning the soul being ruled by the Spirit of God. *"For all who are led by the Spirit are the sons of God"* (Romans 8:14 ESV). This is Sonship.

In my earlier days, I would seek God and wanted to levitate, glow, or have some type of distinguishing sign and wonder that set me apart from everyone else. I would pray, "Lord, make me a glowing saint." I wanted demons to manifest at the sound of my voice. I wanted to heal people with my shadow. This was my goal. Lofty, to say the least, yet now, it is so different. My life-giving glimpses of Jesus and His love have broken me down. I find my prayers are now, "Make me a servant, humble and true. Make me meek, Lord, and lowly like You." For I see that there is where God dwells.

Last year, my wife asked me, "If you could have absolutely anything for your birthday what would it be?" I allowed my mind to limitlessly dream of the possibility of having anything I could ever ask for. As one thing rose after another, I felt a desire for humility rise up in my heart. Then with tears in my eyes, I said, "How much is a humble heart?" To God, the lowly heart is the chief mark of following the lovely Lamb of God. *No one can give you humility but Jesus.* You have to choose to humble yourself. I cannot be humble for you, and you cannot be humble for me.

God is attracted to the kind of humility we see in David. In David, God had found for Himself a man after His own heart in this way—one to whom God was enough (see Acts 13:22). David was one who loved God enough to look at Him. One who loved God enough to wait for Him. One who loved God enough to be stripped down to naked trust. Such nakedness is an invitation for which God unendingly waits. *To be stripped down to nothing invites God to be all.* It's the nakedness of only wanting Him.

The Scripture would suggest to us that David was plucking the strings of God's heart when no man could see. Saul had the people's attention in public, but David had God's attention in private. So, we have a choice ever and always before us: to let go of all others and to have Him only or to hold on to them and be without Him. It's our choice. He won't force you; He'll wait, hoping that soon enough you will get tired and remember Him.

There is a word that has really been in my heart recently. It's the word *only*. Such a small word, but it's very exclusive. Only means there are no others. I've been feeling a song arise in my heart that says, "Only You, Lord, there are no others." *Most people never experience Jesus as all because they never find Him as only.* You'll only experience Him as all that you need when He's the only One you want.

It's all these additions to Him that stop you from being able to experience all of Him. Oh, to only have Him and to only want Him. This is it! David wrote with his poetic pen in Psalm 89:6 that no one can compare to Him. David wrote this in his journal of love.

I pray the Lord would reduce us—reduce us down to Him alone. We cannot refuse this reduction. We must let Him take us back down to only Him. We must be willing to volunteer for such nakedness. Not only is it the state of experiential bliss, but it is also the safest place there is. *We must be a people radically committed to the all-sufficiency of Jesus because every addition is a subtraction from Him.*

CHAPTER 54

Staying within the Cloud

So Moses went into the midst of the cloud...
$\qquad$ (Exodus 24:18 NKJV).

I was in an airport in Seattle, and as I was waiting for my plane to arrive, I observed a plane just after takeoff enter into a cloud. It was absorbed up into the cloud, and the sight of the plane was no more. Such is the swallowing of the life of the believer in the substance of God. The two distinctly different elements become nearly indistinguishable. The lesser is swallowed by the greater. It is difficult to tell where one ends and the other begins.

For the one who seeks union with God, it is simply not enough to merely be around the cloud; there is a burning fire within that wants to go into the cloud. Multitudes stand outside and are content there. But the desperate lover wants to enter the cloud Himself. This lover is convinced and convicted of his deep need of the voice of God. As the psalmist wrote, *"He spoke to them in the cloudy pillar"* (Psalm 99:7 NKJV). God did release His voice from the cloud and around the cloud, but the speaking that is in the cloud is a completely different kind of speaking. The presence around the cloud is wonderful, but it can be penetrated. The experience of His presence is deep, but it can be plunged deeper. His exhilarating voice is reserved for the one who will go in, not satisfied with merely being around His presence, but burning to be absorbed by Him.

Madame Guyon in her commentary on Exodus wrote, "It is the property of God's speaking to absorb our own." God is calling us into the cloud to release His speaking into us—not just to inform us of His desires or educate us in a message, but rather to make us His voice by swallowing us in His own substance. Not just receiving His speaking, but *becoming His speaking.* Notice the lives of the prophets. They became the oracle, the burden. The actual speaking of the prophet issued out of what the prophet was. When John the Baptist was asked who he was, he responded, *"I am 'The voice of one crying in the wilderness…'"* (John 1:23 NKJV). He was God's means of communication to the world. This is what God is after. This is a prophetic generation, a people swallowed by God's own substance.

As we penetrate the presence and the presence penetrates us, His holiness and purity permeate us. The inevitable work of God's nearness is God-likeness. He is Truth and true thoroughly. As the light of His presence exposes our sin, we cast ourselves deeper upon and into Him, who alone makes men holy (see Psalm 90:8). The presence of God has this incredible dichotomous work to it. He will make us holy in His very own presence. *His presence is the workshop of holiness.*

CHAPTER 55

No Deceit in His Mouth

He committed no sin, nor was deceit ever found in His mouth
(1 Peter 2:22 AMP).

Saint Patrick of Ireland wrote:

> ...the lying mouth kills the soul. The same Lord has said in
> the gospel, "on that day of judgment men will have to give
> an explanation for every idle word which they have spoken"
> (Matthew 12:36). Therefore, I ought to worry exceedingly
> with fear and trembling the sentence for that day when none
> can escape or hide and all will have to give an account even of
> the smallest sins before the judgment seat of Christ.[45]

After that striking account from Saint Patrick's confessions, I was
alone in silence for afternoon prayer in a church called Saint Peter and
Paul on the fifteenth day of March. And as the presence of God came
heavily upon me, I was in an instant extremely convicted of the lies I
have implied by remaining silent, or lies of embellishments in story-
telling, or exaggerations for excitement's sake, or simply not telling the
whole truth. So I reached out to the Lord for forgiveness, and as I did
I was granted humility for repentance. When I was repenting, I had a

confirmation of the Spirit by gold dust on my left hand. I felt in my heart to check the date. I remembered it was March 15. As I thought of what the significance could be, the Holy Spirit reminded me of 1 Timothy 3:15 (KJV), *"But if I tarry long, that thou mayest know how thou oughtest to behave thyself in the house of God, which is the church of the living God, the pillar and ground of the truth."*

The church is the "pillar and ground of truth." We must be true. Jesus is the Truth. The Spirit is called the Spirit of Truth. I remember Art Katz saying, "Men seek truths, but God seeks to make us true. The truth is the whole truth and nothing but the truth or it is not the truth at all." So I pray along with Saint Alphonsus Ligouri, "Nail my heart to Your feet, that it may ever remain there, to love You, and never leave You again. I love You more than myself; I repent of having offended You. Grant that I may love You always; and then do with me whatever You will."[46]

We must always remember that apart from Him, we are fountains of wickedness. And that if we leave His embrace our face will turn against Him. Abiding is not just a good idea; if we don't abide we will end up being burned (see John 15:6). However you want to look at that, be it hell, outer darkness, destruction of a life; regardless, it is not a good thing and is a harsh image spoken from the mouth of the Christ for a reason.

CHAPTER 56

Prophets Are Conduits

Son of man, all my words that I shall speak to you receive in your heart, and hear with your ears. And go to the exiles, to your people, and speak to them and say to them "Thus says the Lord God," whether they hear or refuse to hear
(Ezekiel 3:10-11 ESV).

God speaks Himself. Each time God speaks to you He is giving Himself to you. In your maturity as a Christian, you will become exactly whatever God says to you. He forms you by speaking into you. In any peering into prophetic writings, it is easy to note that the lives and words of the prophets are connected to the days in which they are living. As the prophet receives God's words into him, he inevitably becomes God's communication to men. For example, it was God speaking into Hosea coupled with Hosea's obedience that brought Hosea into union with what God was communicating of Himself to him.

It is important to understand that prophets are conduits. They are simply the means of God's message. Hosea embodied God's heartbreak over a people who had covenanted with Him yet refused to love Him. Hosea had come into covenant with a woman who refused loving faithfulness (see Hosea 1:2). Though the prophets themselves personified their divine communication, Hosea's union with his holy relay was unique and arguably the clearest image of God's wounded heart, outside of Christ Himself.

Dear reader, take note. If you feel that such prophetic things are God's desire for your life, you will be united with God's feelings in the same way that Hosea was—God speaking into your soul. If God's voice isn't penetrating your heart, you will never be pierced with His feelings. *If you wish for a prophetic life, you must share both the ecstasy of God and the agony of God.* It is in the enjoyment of His ecstasy that you are enabled to receive and properly steward God's agony. In the name *Hosea*, ecstasy and agony had found a home. Are you willing to house the same? If God gives Himself to us, He will unite our hearts with His agony through the beatific experience of Himself.

CHAPTER 57

My Vision of Hosea—God's Broken Heart

"I will punish her for the days of the Baals to which she burned incense. She decked herself with her earrings and jewelry, and went after her lovers; but Me she forgot," says the Lord
(Hosea 2:13 NKJV).

I remember his face was made of stone, and the expression on his face was deep brokenness. I knew in my spirit that his brokenhearted anguish was a fracture of the kind that only betrayed lovers know. He wasn't God; he was a human possessed with God's feelings. He, himself, in his own body bore God's emotions. By grace, the Lord brought the personification of His current feelings to me through this vision and image of this prophet. In the vision, I knew by intuition that this prophet of stone in front of me was Hosea.

Why was he made of stone? I am not sure. In other instances, the Lord gave messages to prophets and told them that He would make their faces like flint (stone) to break the hardness in His people. I can only speculate that this is what God was trying to communicate to me. Hosea's burden, heart, and message would be relayed and would require a face like flint to break the hardness of God's people.

Prior to this experience, the Spirit had pulled me into a series of profound illuminations through Hosea's prophetic record. Though the

Lord restricted me from speaking of the things that He showed me in those days, I knew that to communicate them would one day be required of me. For more than three years, I waited. Then this vision of a stone Hosea, at the turn of the year 2016, marked what I believe is a distinct disclosing of God's heart toward His people in this time.

Dear reader, many prophets have uttered God's words as divine mouthpieces, but none have pictured for us God's broken heart like what we have seen in Hosea. For though others cry, "Injustice!" "Transgression!" or "Wickedness!" Hosea's nostalgic cry is simply, "You don't love Me anymore."

CHAPTER 58

The Way God Presents Himself

*But rise and stand upon your feet, for I have appeared to you
for this purpose, to appoint you as a servant and witness to the
things in which you have seen me and to those in which I will
appear to you*

(Acts 26:16 ESV).

I have found in my life that it is more important that God has my attention than me knowing what to do. There are often situations where you may be tempted to not be yourself. But I felt like the Lord said to me that, if I change who I am, I cannot accomplish the purpose for which He put me here. And I think that goes for many things in life. *You are right where you are because you are who you are.*

I feel I need to present the Lord in the way that He has presented Himself to me. It's a deep conviction that I carry. So, I can only give to you what He has given of Himself to me. I feel it is very important to say this because people ask me all the time, "Why are you so mushy? Why are you so lovey when you speak about God?"

It's because every time He comes to me, He rushes in like a knight in shining armor rescuing me again, and again, and again! He comes in, and He treats me as if I'm the only one in the room. He is so kind, and

He is so full of love. I'm telling you, *He looks at you as if there is nobody else*. You are a lily among thorns to Him, and He is captivated by you. There is nothing that brings His heart more joy than when you are captivated with Him too. These truths, when realized, begin to strip away our lives of anything that keeps us from Him.

CHAPTER 59

How to Be Faithful

But his delight is in the law of the Lord, and in His law he meditates day and night. He shall be like a tree planted by the rivers of water, that brings forth its fruit in its season, whose leaf also shall not wither; and whatever he does shall prosper (Psalm 1:2-3 NKJV).

Don't we all desire to hear Jesus say to us at the end of our lives, "You were faithful" (see Matthew 25:21)? Wow! Just the thought of the possibility of this moment is tear-jerking. But if being found faithful is deeply desired among God's people, why is it so rare to find a man who lives a faithful life? Even Solomon in his day wrote, *"A faithful man who can find?"* (Proverbs 20:6 KJV).

Is it possible to live our lives faithful to God? Is it possible to live our whole lives thriving with divine life? Yes, I believe it is, and I believe the key to spiritual vitality is found in the first chapter of the book of Psalms. Though many words surround this phrase and lead up to it, the answer is, nonetheless, found in this beautiful string of words, *"whose leaf also shall not wither."*

Whose leaf will not wither? The one who delights in the Lord. What does that mean? It is simply the one who comes to God for satisfaction and consequently finds all his satisfaction in the person of God, that's the one who delights in the Lord, the one who consistently comes to Christ for life.

Imagine a tree that is always green; no matter the weather or the season, it is always lively and flourishing. This is God's chosen imagery to convey to us what His desire is for all of us: He wants us to be trees whose leaves are evergreen, unaffected by all the various seasons of this life. I remember David Popovici saying to me, "Some men are walking revivals." Literally, some men live in a revived state. Isn't this God's desire for us all, to mount up on wings of eagles, and fly above the storms of life and all this world's resistance against the gospel?

God's purpose is that we would live in rich greenness, flourishing right in the face of the oppositions and tribulations of this world! *He wants you and me to be filled with joy in trial and peace in turmoil.* What is salvation if God hasn't given to us His life that is greater than anything that can happen to us during the course of our lives? While everything crumbles around us, in the heat of trials and difficulties, we can remain unaffected.

Oh, dear reader, there is, under His wings, a life that is incorruptible. There is Bread that always satisfies the soul. There is Wine that thrills without fail. There is a living Water of Life that is so glorious that even if we are put in prison, tortured, hated, or framed, we will still thrive! Oh, this wonderful Christ who has given Himself to us as the all-flourishing delight in God!

CHAPTER 60

Staying Childlike

*Truly I say to you, unless you change and become like children,
you will not enter the kingdom of heaven*
(Matthew 18:3 NASB).

A. W. Tozer said, "God discovers Himself to 'babes.' We must simplify our approach to Him. We must strip down to essentials. We must put away all effort to impress and come with the guileless candor of childhood."[47]

When the disciples asked, "Who is the greatest?" Jesus called a child to Himself so that, in the image of the child's coming to Him, He could explain to them what greatness is in the Father's eyes. Wisdom Himself showed them the greatest thing they could do. Dear reader, there is no greatness outside of the greatest thing—Jesus.

Mark tells us that: (1) Jesus called the child; (2) the child came to Him; and (3) Jesus held the child and spoke to His disciples with the child resting upon Him.

Do you see this beautiful imagery? This is how Jesus defined childlikeness: (1) Recognize His desire to be with you; (2) respond to Him by coming to Him; and (3) let Him hold you.

"Who is the greatest?"—would be dissolved by childlikeness. The greatest thing we can do is allow Him to hold us. Jesus said, *"Whoever humbles himself like this child,"* showing us that our response to Him, coming to Him and allowing Him to hold us, are acts of humility (Matthew 18:4 ESV).

Question: What does humility look like?

Answer: It looks like going to Jesus and letting Him hold you.

Jesus didn't suggest this as a better way. He was candid and commanding concerning such a disposition, saying, in effect, "You must be converted like this child."[48] In addition to the illustration Jesus used to correct the disciples' understanding of God and His Kingdom, we can also learn much from the fact that Jesus used a child to demonstrate His instruction. We know by this that there are certain characteristics, for the most part, distinct to children that will unfold more for us concerning what Jesus wants us to be.

Children provide nothing for themselves. I ask you, who is the most cared for in any home? Is it not the youngest? Who receives the most attention in the house? It is, without a doubt, the youngest.

John Wesley wrote, "Little children are lowly at heart, and they know themselves utterly ignorant and helpless and hang upon their Father in Heaven to supply all of their needs." The childlike heart is honest with itself about itself. The childlike heart lives in recognition of always needing the Father. Childlikeness is to have a habitual consciousness of our insufficiency. We must live recognizing that He is the only One who can provide for us. Logic cannot make it happen; you cannot twist or manipulate things into your own favor. We can only bow before the Lord with an uncovered heart—not puffed up concerning ourselves, but looking to the Father.

Andrew Murray wrote, "The true beauty of childlikeness is the absence of self-consciousness." Could it be that hearing the disciples' hearts caused Jesus to point out a child for that very reason? Maybe to be a child means not thinking less of others when you are made higher than them, and not envying others when they are made higher than you. "Who then is greatest in the Kingdom of heaven?" Children are different from this. Jesus was saying, in effect, "Children receive the Kingdom, and this one thing is sure: They do not think like you do."

The disciples sought greatness, not by character but by name. This is what Jesus was correcting. It is when our names are in our view that we have grown apart from Him. When our names are in view, we begin to ask, "Who is the greatest in the Kingdom?" This is not the lowly heart that follows the lowly Lamb.

Being converted means having a different mind about yourself and a different mind about His Kingdom than what comes naturally to us. Peter was the chief speaker. He must have assumed he would be Lord-Chancellor in the Kingdom. Simon and Jude were nearly related to Christ. They must have expected to be heavenly princes by blood. Judas held the money bag. He may have thought of himself as the head treasurer in the courts of Heaven. Andrew was the first called. He would have easily thought that he was first place.

By bringing a child in their midst, Jesus rebuked their corrupt intent. He destroyed selfish ambition, pride, self-centeredness, making a name and the need to be recognized as something great. Jesus is so different from any other. *Men look to sit on a throne; God wants men to sit on His knee.* Children on His knee say, "My Father will take care of this for me."

CHAPTER 61

Elkanah and Hannah

There was a certain man from Ramathaim-zophim of the hill country of Ephraim whose name was Elkanah.... He had two wives. The name of the one was Hannah, and the name of the other, Peninnah. And Peninnah had children, but Hannah had no children

(1 Samuel 1:1-2 ESV).

In the day and culture in which Elkanah and Hannah lived, a woman found her identity and dignity in bearing children. Her main role was to give her husband children, especially a son to carry on the father's name and line. The fruitfulness of her womb was the culture's only measure of success and value for her.

Elkanah's other wife, Peninnah, had a fruitful womb. Her "production" testified to her culture that she was a successful wife, and her "productivity" was her confidence. Having many children awarded her dignity, identity, and praise, removing the pressure of the culture's thought patterns off her shoulders. Her fruitfulness gave evidence as a prideful witness that she had proven herself in accordance with her culture.

Hannah, on the other hand, though she was greatly loved, was barren and had the pressure of the culture constantly weighing down on her. Obviously, the provocative testimony of the other wife was internally vexing, degrading, and humiliating (see 1 Samuel 1:6). Hannah suffered such emotional pressure and humiliation that she was sick to her stomach and could not eat (see 1 Samuel 1:7).

The mindset of the culture demanded that she produce something that she was simply unable to do. This constant tension broke her soul. She was distraught and oppressed by the cultural traditions, but most of all, Hannah was shamed by Peninnah's fruitful life.

Peninnah provoked her, but the power she had over Hannah did not come from Peninnah herself, but rather from the patterns of thinking in their culture. Ultimately, Hannah was oppressed by the voice of human demand, human systems, and human traditions.

Do you relate to Hannah? Are you depressed and frustrated with your ministry, judging its success by the numbers (of salvations, of healings, of responses) or results? Are you burdened because your ministry is not growing or frustrated because the unsaved haven't submitted to the gospel through your witness? If there is any competition hidden in your veins, or any jealousy harbored in your soul, keep reading. I promise that Jesus will eradicate it through one phrase.

CHAPTER 62

Elkanah and Jesus

Then Elkanah her husband said to her, "Hannah, why do you weep? Why do you not eat? And why is your heart grieved? Am I not better to you than ten sons?"

(1 Samuel 1:8 NKJV)

When Hannah came to her husband, he gave the greatest portrayal of the heart of Jesus Christ that there could be in this situation by saying, *"Am I not better to you than ten sons?"* It is almost as if he was hurt by the fact that something else was the measure of her life.

These words reveal to us that, in his great love for Hannah, Elkanah looked for the reason why she was not fulfilled by his love alone. He asked her, "Am I not of more value to you than many children?" Ten is a great number because it represents completion, and as stated earlier, sons are the greatest fruit a woman can have in their culture. Elkanah was asking his oppressed wife in her frustration, "Am I not more to you than all the fruit in the world?"

My dear friend, this is the heart of Jesus. In the same way, He asks: "Are you not fulfilled in Me? Am I not enough? Am I not all sufficient? Am I not I AM? Is fruit or are results more precious to you than I am? Why do you need something more than Me to be happy, satisfied, or delighted? My heart hurts because you are not fulfilled by My love."

I believe some of our frustrated prayers break God's heart, for they reveal to Him that He is no longer the center of our hearts. Jesus' heart is broken by much of our ambition for results, for it replaces Him as the source and joy of life. To be loved by you is the goal of His loving you.

Elkanah gave Hannah such a shocking love that existed outside the thought processes of man. His love found value in her without demanding fruitfulness as the culture did; his love wanted her to be satisfied only with him; in his love, the couple needed nothing more than each other.

CHAPTER 63

Hannah's Transformation

Then Hannah rose after eating and drinking in Shiloh. Now Eli the priest was sitting on the seat by the doorpost of the temple of the Lord. She, greatly distressed, prayed to the Lord and wept bitterly. She made a vow and said, "O Lord of hosts, if You will indeed look on the affliction of Your maidservant and remember me, and not forget Your maidservant, but will give Your maidservant a son, then I will give him to the Lord all the days of his life, and a razor shall never come on his head"

(1 Samuel 1:9-11 NASB1995).

In response to such a loving statement from her husband that proved he only wanted her for herself, she stopped weeping, got up, found her appetite, and communed with her husband at the table. *The sad fact is that much of our crying for fruit has robbed us of sweet communion with Jesus.* And though in the next verse she again cried for fruitfulness, her tears were different; we find a subtle change that makes all the difference in the entire world.

She still pleaded for a son, the best fruit, but now it was for a totally different reason. Her motive changed and was purified. While her first cries came from the painful weight of the system of man that wrapped her identity and dignity in productivity and fruitfulness, her last cry was simply to have fruit to be able to give to God. She wanted to bear the best fruit to be able to offer at the feet of God Himself.

She was no longer bound by thinking of her own face and testifying of her own life in accordance with the system of the culture, speaking man's language of success, beating herself for lack of fruit, and comparing her life to others.

Now she was free to find all her joy in her husband and not worry if he would leave her if she is unable to produce. Now she cried to God for the right reason, lifting up her tears in purity and weeping out of selflessness. She no longer wanted fruit to validate herself; she wanted fruit to present to God, to give something of value to Him, instead of seeking to be valued by her culture.

One may say, "The Scripture stated earlier that God had closed her womb, so her fruitlessness was because of God." Exactly! Sometimes God prevents us from bearing the fruit that we want so that He can look into our eyes and say, "Am I not more to you than ten sons?" When God spoke this to me personally, He broke me out of a bondage that I didn't even know I was in, breaking me into a realm of freedom, rest, and ease beyond anything I could have ever thought possible—a realm where the literal joy of Heaven and the wine of the Spirit could be consumed for the right reason: intimate union.

A preacher who is looking for more signs and wonders; a pastor who wants a building; an evangelist who desires to see more numbers; a teacher who wants more committed students—whatever your frustration for productivity might be, in your frustration listen to the heart of your Bridegroom, for it beats this lovely phrase, "Am I not more to you than those things? Am I not enough for you? Am I not more to you than money? Am I not more to you than miracles? Am I not more to you than souls being saved? Am I not more to you than apparent fruitfulness?"

This issue must be settled first: If we are ever to pray with a pure cry, we must be satisfied with Him alone. If we ever want to be pure enough to simply desire to lay fruit at His feet, we must find such contentment with His simple love and presence, forsaking the longings for our own significance.

This issue of being satisfied with God alone will open our hearts to offer to Jesus our substance. Hannah said, "I will give him to You all the days of his life." Her heart cried, "This fruit is not for my name; no one will even see me with him. This fruit is not to remove my disgrace and shame or to give me dignity or identity. It is all for You, and You alone." We will be forever set free from the oppressive demand for production when we settle in our hearts that Jesus alone in our lives in daily experience is enough to satisfy everything that we could ever desire. *He is enough!*

CHAPTER 64

Exhausting the Riches of Jesus Christ

I have been crucified with Christ; it is no longer I who live, but Christ lives in me

(Galatians 2:20 NKJV).

Frank Viola, Christian author, blogger, and speaker, was asked, "What will you do when other thoughts, or other doctrines, or teachings, or traditions start crowding in on your fellowship?" He replied, "I will tell them this, 'We will respond to those things after we have exhausted the riches of Jesus Christ.'"

I am afraid that we are in danger of eclipsing our dependency upon the experiential, abiding fellowship in Jesus with the truth concerning our identity in Him. It seems we have become so taken with what He has made us that we no longer recognize our desperate need of Him, not only in our teaching but also in our daily lives. *Is it possible that by looking so intently at who we are in Him, we have shifted our gaze from Him?*

How do we endure in this life? Is it by looking at ourselves or by looking to Jesus? Author of *Tortured for Christ* Richard Wurmbrand said, "The 'I' must be abolished. 'I no longer live,' not the old Paul, not the new Paul, but Christ lives in me." In fact, the anthem of the new nature should be, "Worthy is the Lamb."

Our identity in Christ is wrapped up in looking at Jesus in worship, depending upon Jesus, and receiving from Him our daily bread, waiting and abiding with Him as submitted children. The new nature recognizes that, without Him, we can do nothing and are helpless. Such a mindset was impossible for the old nature, but now we are taught to recollect spiritual truths concerning ourselves, that knowing the facts about what Christ has made us is the basis for victorious living.

Something is wrong when I am not taught to run into Jesus during times of difficulty, but just to remind myself who I am. The spiritual life does not stem from learning the facts about my new self, but rather forgetting about myself when I look at Him. *Looking at my identity causes me to look away from Him.*

The new nature should be captivated by Him, by hearing His voice and experiencing His presence in daily life. The last thing the new nature will do is talk about itself, for even the Holy Spirit will not testify of Himself, but only of the Son. As a matter of fact, our new outlook should be to overlook ourselves so that we might see Him.

The only Source of life is Jesus, and the perpetual gaze upon Him is the all-sufficient universal solution for everything in the life of a believer. *Christ will not share the throne of your heart with you.*

I am not saying that this wave is satanic or devilish, but I am saying that it is dangerous because it reminds me of a distraction that took place before the beginning of time. Lucifer, "perfect and beautiful," was the handiwork of God. As an anointed angel, God placed him on the earth with some level of authority. But when he began to exalt what God had made him, he was banned; he began perfect, and self-focus was enough to disqualify him from the glory of God.

Vance Havner said, "If Christ didn't come to save us from self-infatuation, I don't know what the Savior came to do." He didn't save us from self-infatuation to bring us into a sanctified form of the same. David Popovici said to me, "It seems in the lives of many Christians that the self-life is still king; he just changed his outfit."

Even ministers I deeply respect are subtly shifting their focus. The other day, a minister that has greatly touched my life said, "When the

I AM takes residence in you, you are able to say, 'I am,'" teaching that the evidence of God's presence is a revelation of self. This is askew. The evidence of the residence of the I AM is a life that proclaims, "HE IS!"

Moses' encounter with the I AM produced a greater dependency on God. In essence, Moses was saying, "If You don't go with me, I don't go"; and when his face shone with glory, "he knew not" (see Exodus 33:15). Gideon was called "a mighty man of valor" simply because he didn't see himself as one (Judges 6:12). Paul wrote in 2 Corinthians 4:5 (NKJV), *"We do not preach ourselves, but Christ Jesus the Lord...."* A great man of God once told me, "Many people cannot recognize God's presence because they are too busy recognizing their own presence."

There are many examples of this mentality in the Western church that I could point out, but rather let me just state what we need to see: *Jesus is all.* Anything that is preached or emphasized to pump us into frenzy about what we are in God is distorted identity. Pure identity in Christ is Christ. *True identity in Christ is the exaltation and proclamation of Christ's great worth and glory.*

After searching the Scriptures, I see that there is very little reference to self-awareness in the new life. We are not taught in Paul's letters a recollection practice any more than a doctor would tell a woman who wants to have children to remind herself she is pregnant. The only way to conceive the things that God wants to birth into the earth is to intimately experience Jesus. It is a life of coming unto Him that causes us to produce fruit.

In an intimate experience with my wife, the last thing I would do is confess to myself who I am. Rather, I would allow myself to be captivated by her beauty and preoccupied with my desire for her. This is our identity—a people endlessly preoccupied with God Himself.

Men quickly fall in love with their own legacies—this statement seems to be truer among Christians than anywhere else. We claim to be driven to "make an impact," but the closer others draw to our hearts, it seems to cover the lust for our own name and legacy. *Our selfish humanity leads us to a hidden desire and a secret passion for our own personal significance.*

We constantly announce our activities, results, and stories in our own ministries, but in reality, we are just manifesting our Adamic pursuit for significance. I understand that the only way to tell people what is going on is to tell them what is going on, but it seems that under the guise of "identity in Christ" and "being fruitful," we have found a justification for exalting ourselves.

Does our faith rest upon what we think ourselves to be in God, or are we content to remain nothing before God that He may show Himself strong? If this is accurate, this just indicates our failure to be wholly satisfied with His sweet presence in us, with just being His, and with loving Him and receiving His love every day.

CHAPTER 65

The Whisper of the Bridegroom

I charge you, O daughters of Jerusalem, if you find my beloved, that you tell him I am lovesick!
(Song of Solomon 5:8 NKJV).

My prayer is that you find a "secret unction" hidden under these words that will compel you to taste and enjoy the Bridegroom in a way far beyond your wildest imagination of holy romance. As God's ultimate desire is to dispense His own life into His creatures through *communing* with the words of His heart, I am convinced that God will lavish His perfect love upon you through this unlearned and foolish heart of mine.

In recent weeks, my heart felt that "holy itch" to write again, but I had no idea what He wanted me to write; so, I waited. Oh precious one, did you notice that last sentence? Waiting is the divine sifting in which God can remove the dross-filled desire for attention, significance, and the terrible plague of human reasoning that offers to God things that are so contrary to His nature that He cannot, and never will, accept them. *Waiting pulls the whisper of the Bridegroom toward the ear of our soul.*

Something in the deepest part of me is crying out! *The Holy Spirit is trying His best to introduce the body of Christ to the Living Bridegroom.* But it seems to me that our hearts are set on everything else but Him.

You see it is not about falling on the floor. It is not about preaching. It is not about evangelizing. It is not about pastoring. It is not about buildings. It is not about money. It is about the Lord Jesus Christ.

I can hear John Kilpatrick, who had pastoral oversight of the historic Brownsville Revival, saying in my heart to the Lord, "I want You. I don't want religion. I don't want another church. I don't want another congregation. I don't want another Bible. I don't want another wife. I don't want more kids. I want You, Lord!"

Dear reader, we must have Jesus. Jesus alone! His presence! Just Him. Only Him. *Precious Bridegroom, captivate our hearts again!*

As I waited for a few months before writing a word, pushing away the urge simply to fill a page with truths and clever articulations, God met me in a wonderful way. This life-changing personal experience is what has birthed these pages. You might ask, "What does your personal experience have to do with my life?" I know that God's nature is to take the words herein that He has spoken into me, and the experiences that He has thrust upon me, to pull you into a greater, more profound experience of His Son.

Whether you are thriving in God or barely surviving in God, this lovesick treatise will aid the health of your soul. To borrow the words of A. W. Tozer, "If my fire is not large, it is yet real, and there may be those who can light their candle at its flame."

Pray this with me. Precious Living Bridegroom, make Yourself audible to my heart, tangible to my spirit and visible to my soul that I may love You more than I do now.

CHAPTER 66

An Infection of Affection

...I am lovesick

(Song of Solomon 2:5 NKJV).

Nearly three weeks before writing this, I experienced an intense season of "sickness of love." I use the word *intense* simply because, for my poor soul, it was nothing short of extreme. What I am about to describe may not seem intense to another, but what I write, nonetheless, is an attempt to convey, from my heart, even to the smallest degree, what sometimes happens in the life of someone who seeks to live in holy lovesickness.

Such a sickness of love is a desire so intensely singular that it is unable to be satisfied or content, or to even experience moments of happiness apart from the loved one. To apply these words to the case of holy lovesickness, it is a Spirit-produced love eruption in the soul such that it is unable to enjoy anything independent of God. For the lovesick, any enjoyable thing must first pass through Him.

During this time of extreme lovesickness, my stomach felt constantly sick, not physically, but deep inside my soul existed a rumbling that I could only describe as life-swallowing death. Although it did not physically hurt, there was what I can only describe as a sort of inward bleeding. It was akin to a "spiritual bereavement" coupled with a strange consciousness and desire for God, so overwhelming that I was unable to eat. Bereavement can be defined as an irretrievable loss of something held dear.

This is the best way to describe it. I was without appetite, and nothing passed through my mouth for days. Yet it was nothing like fasting. Fasting is intentional and dedicated to God. This was not that. This simply happened to me. I did not schedule it. It merely happened; He seized me to Himself.

During these days, I also could not sleep through the night. I would wake up, caused by the overwhelming sense of God's love and presence, cry for a little while, and then go back to sleep only to have this experience repeated several times each night. I couldn't function because I was in a constant state of ecstatic meditation or adoration that brought with it a deluge of love and the inebriating consciousness of Him into my soul.

I wept constantly. The hallways, kitchen, living room, car, closet, and pillows were wet with tears, tears from a broken heart aching for God. The psalmist writes of such a craving using the words, *"My soul thirsts for you"* (Psalm 63:1 NKJV). What an incredible string of words. Think of the meaning of these words.

In essence, this verse says, "My soul [all that I am] is pining [literally aches] for nothing other than You." It was Saint Teresa of Avila who explained this pining as, "My soul suffers out of desire for Him." Lovesickness in the soul may, at times, be accompanied with seasons of intensified acute aching, throbbing with love and longing to simply groan, gaze, and adore. You may know exactly what I experienced. I pray that as you read this description it would remind your heart of some of your own wonderful seasons of intense love exchange with Jesus.

Though these were days full of random emotional breakdowns in which I was overcome with such a love craving for Him that I looked as if I lost my dearest loved one, they were also permeated with blissful currents of what felt like a river of honey flowing over, in, and around me. I'm not sure what was actually happening to me. But somehow, I knew these were deep workings of the Spirit in my soul. What they performed in my heart was worth more than a million years of exhaustive theology or the self-imposed "chiseling of spiritual disciplines."

Forgive my redundancy, but all that I do know is that my heart was aching with love for Him whose heart aches for us. *"Deep calls unto deep"* is the language that comes to mind (Psalm 42:7 NKJV). To one degree or another, such aching should be part of our lives. This is lovesickness. He calls us closer. He beckons us upon the waters of His love. He whispers to come away to the wilderness, where no other voice can be heard.

Close your eyes for ten seconds and listen with your heart, whoever and wherever you are. Don't feel discouraged if you are unfamiliar with what I am talking about. I am aware that, though lovesickness is the bride's way of life, the intensity of seasons like the one I just passed through are uncommon to most people. But one thing is undeniably true—such seasons are available to everyone. This is why you are reading this book. He beckons you.

I also know that these times of great intensity are periodic. Why? Simply because such a state of brokenheartedness that robs sleep and appetite makes it impossible to sustain a marriage, a family, a job, or even physical life. This is not God's desire. *His desire is to seize you to Himself and make you a fountain of grace for your family and those you with whom you come into contact.*

I recall the words of the deceased prophet Arthur Katz, "Jesus refused any fulfillment or gratification independent of His Father." Jesus—perfect lovesick Son that He was—shows us the glistening morning dew resting on His head as He daily chose the place of solitude with His Father. He was drawn, literally inwardly pulled by love, to rest upon His Father and have every element of His life issue from that quiet place of solitude. This is the only place where the lovesick heart finds enjoyment and consolation, *"Let His left hand be under my head and His right hand embrace me"* (Song of Solomon 2:6 AMP). To experience the bosom of the Father is life itself, and to remain there is perfected godliness. *That inexplicable craving to lay upon His chest is lovesickness.* Holiness is simply the lifestyle of the lovesick. For true holiness can be summed up in statements such as, *"I shall not want,"* or, *"There is none upon earth that I desire besides You"* (Psalm 23:1; 73:25 NKJV). Oh, the lovesick soul sees Him alone. *There is a seeing that induces holy blindness.*

The phrase *lovesick* expresses the same love that we see scripted by the lover's pen dripping with love better than wine in the Song of Solomon. It expresses the sensual and experiential love exchange between two love-stricken, single-eyed persons, whose lives are marked by an overwhelming craving for unbroken union with each other.

Lovesickness teaches us that love exchange with Jesus is far too beautiful to give our attention elsewhere. Lovesickness teaches that it is far better to give attention to Him, who causes fruit, than to give attention to the development of any single aspect of fruit. Lovesickness teaches us that the highest of all is in His person alone. *Lovesickness is the greatest safeguard against the carnal and all those religious substitutions for Jesus.* Sometimes we think something is important. It may be a teaching or a revelation or a perspective, or a ritual or a manifestation of some kind. But whatever it is, it pales in comparison to His person seen, heard, touched, and experienced.

CHAPTER 67

The Longing of the Son

The Spirit and the bride say, "Come!"

(Revelation 22:17 NKJV)

In Revelation 22:17, we read the last time that we, the Church, are mentioned in Scripture. Look at it again. What are we called? We are called *the bride*. Notice, it doesn't say warriors. It doesn't say soldiers. It doesn't say theologians. It says bride. When He returns, He is looking for something specific from us. What does a bridegroom want from His bride? Love. *Loving Jesus is the heart and soul of Christianity*.

The Scriptures show us that when He comes, He comes as the shining Bridegroom to have His bride (see Matthew 25:1). He is not coming as anything else. He is coming to get married (see Revelation 19:9). We will be the wife of the Lamb (see Revelation 21:9). We all have read this, but I feel that it is time for these truths to sink into our bones. It is one thing for truth to be in the brain, but it is a completely different experience when it drops into the blood. I pray that you would be thoroughly convinced with each heartbeat that you belong to Him, and no other.

The Bridegroom and the bride are not only symbolic of Christ and the Church, but Christ and the individual soul. When we see this wonderful, romantic, giddy, sweet, love exchange between Bridegroom and bride, we see God's intended and desired relationship with you and your heart. Man's common concept of God is that He desires man for His use, but the Bible clearly reveals that God desires man for union. *Our inner life is to be baptized in first love and to have a heart racing for Him that makes His heart race.*

I declare unto you, though I am not a prophet, nor am I the son of a prophet, soon every message that you hear and every book that is printed in the Christian genre will be about the Bridegroom. For many years, the Church at large has had her eyes on everything else; this stream emphasizes this and that stream emphasizes that. Yet, soon, all will narrow down to One sight: the Bridegroom. This is where everything is headed. It will be upon all lips. The tongue will speak of the poetry of love. Soon, the Song of Solomon will be understood and experienced by every Christian. It's the book that's been most rejected, taken for granted, and looked over. Yet, soon, people won't be able to get away from it, for this is where everything is headed—loving Jesus like the bride loves the Bridegroom.

I cannot tell you how many times I've been written to and rebuked for romanticizing Christ. Yet, He has made Himself romantic. This is not something that Eric Gilmour came up with. Certainly, the paternal revelation paints a vivid image and is used and valued in the Scriptures, but the way that I see the Scriptures, the bridal relationship still excels the paternal. Why? Children come from you without choice. The bride is the joining of two into one. You can understand aspects of divine love through children, but the highest of all is bride and Bridegroom. It means you have chosen, by love, to give up yourself for another.

It's been preordained and sown into the fabric of time that God loves you and wants you. The way He chose to explain it to you was by setting up a man attracted with burning love for a woman and a woman absolutely satisfied in a man. This understanding of loving Him with all our hearts is not new. It stands as holy bookends at the very beginning and the very end. How do we know this? In the very first book of the Bible, the stage is set, *"For this reason a man shall leave his father and his mother, and be joined to his wife; and they shall become one flesh"*

(Genesis 2:24 AMP). Many want to overlook this, but it is written by God Himself. His premise in the very beginning was non-negotiable, and it's this—it's a love story, a man being given a woman. It's the starting place of humanity and the ground for the display of His manifold wisdom. *God's desired revelation for mankind is displayed in His decision to give Adam a bride.*

The act of two becoming one means the loss of self in another. This is bridal, to leave all else behind and find ourselves in another. So, they, Adam and Eve, had each other in the garden called "pleasure." This is the origin of the story of God's plan to unveil His son to humanity and simultaneously reveal to humanity what kind of relationship He desires to have. *"So also it is written, 'The first man, Adam, became a living soul.' The last Adam became a life-giving spirit"* (1 Corinthians 15:45 AMP). Jesus is the last Adam. The first Adam was given a bride. The last Adam is given a bride. Adam in Genesis is a shadow of the substance of the last Adam, Jesus. It was preordained that you would be able to read about Adam and Eve as a shadow to Jesus and His bride.

It is interesting to note that you can see my shadow, but you cannot know me by my shadow. You've got to know my substance to know me. Likewise, Adam is merely a shadow of the substance of the Man, Christ Jesus. Eve is simply a shadow of you. Paul galvanizes these truths later in Ephesians by quoting Genesis and expounding upon it writing, *"For this reason a man shall leave his father and mother and be joined to his wife, and the two shall become one flesh.' This mystery is great, but I am speaking with reference to Christ and the church"* (Ephesians 5:31-32 NKJV).

Bridal love is when our love for Him causes a "What can I do to please You, Lord?" to rise in our hearts. This shifts the paradigm from being whipped into obedience to falling in love and giving ourselves to the desires of Another. This is the nature of love. It is easy to let go of yourself for the one that you love.

You are the bride that Jesus is head over heels for. He wants all your attention, and everything you are looking for is found in giving Him the attention He wants from you. That is the gospel: He loves you and is taken with you. He didn't just love you upon the cross when He bled for you. *He loves you right now.*

DELIGHTING IN HIS PRESENCE

Even as you read this, I beg you, on behalf of the Lord, do not be content to merely hear the knocking of His holy hand upon the door of your heart. Yield. Open up to Him. He is your loving Bridegroom. Yes, just put the book down and with all sincerity and vulnerability of heart say, "Please, come in, my Precious Lover. Precious Jesus, don't wait outside. Come live in me. Make me Your home today and always."

If you will daily give Him time to come in, I promise, He will daily sweep you off your feet and hold you in a way that will heal and fill your soul in areas you didn't even know needed healing and filling. His touch will forever damage you beyond repair. He will unite Himself with your soul in a highly experiential way. I am learning over and over that in yielding we may look like fools, but that is the life of the lovesick. *A holy bride is wholly His.*

CHAPTER 68

His Starry-Eyed Bride

I am my beloved's, and his desire is toward me
(Song of Solomon 7:10 NKJV).

Many search their entire lives for such a union. *Soul mate*, as it is called, is just another term expressing the deep desire of humanity to be fulfilled. We who have laid our hearts at the feet of Christ know a satisfaction far more delightful than mere human union.

For God became a Man yet remained God. Jesus is the holy name of that unfathomable merger. And with Him, we have the fullest union and most delightful experience of complete love.

The bride in Song of Solomon spoke of being her lover's current possession. *"I am my beloved's,"* free from the restless anticipation of "maybe someday" or the wearying uncertainty of performing to obtain Him as a reward; she was then His.

She was settled. No more racing. No more chasing. She could rest in His arms. Fully His. Accepted. *"I am my beloved's."* She was not her own. Her desires were not for herself anymore. She saw her future was His. Her passions were His. Her mind and will were His. She was gladly owned. If such a thought was not sufficient to bring joy unspeakable into the soul, she spoke further: *"His desire is for me."*

We know what it is to desire something. God has installed in us such a capability. We have all sought ways to obtain things we want. We have arranged life in certain ways to obtain certain ends. We have put ourselves "through the mill" at times, moved by such a force as desire. God has installed this. He did so seeking to explain how He feels toward us. For having installed desire and made its deep feeling known to us in everyday life, He says through Jeremiah, *"I have loved you with an everlasting love..."* (Jeremiah 31:3 NKJV). He desires us.

He has suffered Himself in order to seek us out and win our love. And that is all. The bride did not mention His desire for something from her. She knew His desire was for her. For her person. Not for her services. Not for her land or money or heritage or help. He had looked at her in such a way. Her blushing face said, "He wants me." No doubts or additions. He desired her. He was all-in for her. None have desired you so.

To be desired by someone is wonderful; and God Himself is far more than our minds could ever grasp. Millennia upon millennia will expound upon such a truth to our hearts. Even angels ask, *"What is man that You are mindful of him...?"* (Psalm 8:4 NKJV).

Reader, you are loved. Don't allow anyone to dissuade you from security in His arms. Refuse to listen to anything not fragrant with His desire for you. Daily set your heart higher than the world and all other loves by saying, "I am my Beloved's, and His desire is for me."

CHAPTER 69

His Kiss, Your Cure

Let him kiss me with the kisses of his mouth—for your love is better than wine

(Song of Solomon 1:2 NKJV).

God lacks a filter between His heart and His lips. He loves in kisses. What do I mean by that? I mean He longs to directly contact you intimately and lovingly, repeatedly. See, if we take experience out of our relationship with God, all we have left is an idea. That experience is a sweet and tender kiss from God. French abbot and mystic Bernard of Clairvaux said, "The kiss is a participation in the life and love of the trinity. We are made one by this so we rest in rapture, which is the key of His mouth."[49]

In Song of Solomon, the entire romantic exchange between the bride and the groom is founded with and starts with, *"Let him kiss me with the kisses of his mouth."* This loving, intimate, direct contact with God is the experience of love. How do we know this? Because she goes on to say, *"Your love is better than wine."* These kisses of His love are what the Scriptures are calling us into; to be directly contacted by God. We, as blood-bought believers, have access to the sweet kiss of God, yet we often forget such things. Yet the lover in Song of Solomon loves ardently because she is drunk with love. She is overcome by Him.

The kiss will keep us. It thrills us and matures us. The bride looks for kisses before words. Sometimes we forget how important it really is to receive the sweet nothings of God that satisfy our soul.

He is longing for those who will stare at Him and let the grin in His eyes linger inside them. Who will look at Him, lean in, and be kissed? Kissed in such a way that whenever you lean out, you feel Him pulling you back in again? How do you know what the kiss is? I'll tell you this: *The kiss is when you can feel in your heart the Holy Spirit saying something like this, "Don't leave. No, not yet. Stay with me."*

You may know exactly what I am referring to. Perhaps you felt it this morning in prayer. Perhaps the sweetness was overtaking you, and you felt as though God was holding you, pleading for you to stay with Him. The kiss can turn any location into a garden of spices with your Beloved. When He kisses you, He leaves gardens in your soul that reproduce after their own kind. He loves you and wants all of you.

Sometimes you look around and say, "All this stuff is right in the midst of Christianity, but something is missing." *Most of the time, what's missing is the kissing.* There might be a lot of things, but there is no cure like God's kiss. His kiss can cure your evil and bring you to His bliss and give you Him for whom you sigh, Jesus your sweetness. His kiss will kill competition. His kiss will kill condemnation. His kiss will kill comparison, and you will be free. Most of our issues can be solved right there. So much of the pain we experience in this life is the absence of the kiss. Whenever a friend comes to me for advice or counsel of any kind my first question is, "When was your last kiss?" Pray with me, *Lord, I was lost before Your kiss, and now I'm lost without Your kisses.*

CHAPTER 70

The Beauty of the Bridegroom

What kind of beloved is your beloved, O most beautiful among women?

(Song of Solomon 5:9 NASB)

There is a fictional story that says the apostles had seen Jesus in His fullness and His awesome power. They watched and marveled as He spoke and acted—full of God, for He was God. They ran to get Nathanael and longed to introduce Nathanael to Jesus. As they went on the way, Nathanael said, "What is He like?"

Peter said, "His face was so, so powerful."

John said, "No, no, no, it was His voice. His voice was so rich."

Then James interjected and said, "We don't know what it was. We just know that He is supernatural." They didn't have any words to describe Him.

Nathanael shot back, "I don't believe in things like that."

John replied, "Oh, you will when you see Him."

See, every time I see Him, I am convicted of forgetting how beautiful He really is. When you see Him, yes, He will captivate your heart, yet His character is of such a variety that you could fall in love with Him with your eyes closed! *God's design was never to corner men and collect their consent, but rather to captivate their hearts by displaying the beauty of His own nature.*

The bride was asked a specific question in our opening verse, *"What kind of beloved is your beloved?"* I want to now expound upon the incredible description she gives of Him. I can't help but see the blind world wondering about the Man we all worship. "What is so special about Jesus?" She called Him her *"beloved." Beloved* means one who is loved, the one I love, the one who holds my affections, the one who has taken my heart, the one who has held me captive by his charms. She was very certain of her love for him, and she went on to describe him in detail.

CHAPTER 71

Brightness Extreme and a Bleeding Dream

My beloved is dazzling and ruddy…
(Song of Solomon 5:10 NASB1995).

The word *dazzling* means He is stunning. To be dazzled is to have the consciousness of your surroundings temporarily suspended by the brightness of beauty. Imagine, while you are reading this book a bright light hits you and you become blind to the book, your surroundings, and everything else by brightness extreme. Whatever happens around you falls behind and you cannot see around you anymore because you have been overcome in your perception.

This is what happened to Saul in Acts 9. Jesus appeared in His resplendent glory, in a sense, almost asking Paul to marry Him. And Paul responded with the fitting words of the bride; just as Sarah did, calling her husband, Abraham, "Lord" (see Genesis 18:12; 1 Peter 3:6).

The bride's response to the question of His beauty is specifically pointing our attention to the fact that our Bridegroom is light, which means He is God who is Light (see 1 John 1:5).

Now notice the word *ruddy*. This word means the color of blood. Do you see what she is doing? She is describing our Christ! He is brightness extreme, yet He is the color of blood. What is the significance of this? He is the radiance of God, divine. Yet He is bleeding. He is brightness extreme, and the bleeding dream. He is too bright to see, yet He bleeds for me. He is the perfection of glory, combined with humanity. The highest of angels cannot gaze into His light unapproachable, and no human can stomach the naked blood of His humiliation.

As mentioned previously, I programmed my Alexa device to respond to my, "Good morning," with, "Eric, remember the gospel. He is enough. Love Him. He alone is worthy." It is a daily reminder that He alone is God—Creator of Heaven and earth. He is all-knowing, all-powerful, yet He became a human being (see John 1:14). He subjected His glorious, limitless person to the restrictions and frailties of a human body. His meekness and majesty cannot be compared to another. May He help us believe this, for in it we see His beauty.

CHAPTER 72

"Chiefest among Ten Thousand"

My beloved...is outstanding among ten thousand
(Song of Solomon 5:10 NIV).

The bride cannot contain herself as she burst out this love statement hardly rivaled by any of the greatest love poets known to men. The King James Version of this verse renders it, *"My beloved is...the chiefest among ten thousand."* Charles Spurgeon noted, "There is no such word as chiefest." Such is the weight of Christ's perfections—He breaks down vocabulary and causes men to say words they have never known to articulate something they have never seen.

Andrew Murray echoed, "Everything depends upon God taking the chief place." This idea applies to everything: your marriage, evangelism, prayer, the Bible, and beyond. Biblical commentaries have noted that *chiefest* is described as being a flag of distinction. He is the standard—the One everything falls under. The rallying point. The Mount Zion of God. God's chosen King (see Psalm 45). The appearance of the Bridegroom is distinguished above all. Mary's oil marks Him as the greatest in the room (see John 12).

You might wonder, *He is chiefest among ten thousand? Ten thousand what?* He is chiefest among ten thousand of anything you want. Ten thousand shepherds cannot compare to the Good Shepherd. Ten thousand preachers stand mute in sight of the Living Word. Ten thousand angels bow before the Captain of the hosts of the Lord. Ten thousand warriors lay their swords before the King of kings and Lord of lords. Ten thousand lovers cannot win your heart like Jesus. He is your Bridegroom. He is your beautiful King. Why do we love Him? Look at how beautiful He is. He is the One from start to finish—the highest and the lowest.

Following her comment on Him being chiefest, she moved into describing His beauty. In verse 11 (NKJV) she says, *"His head is like the finest gold."* The word *head* can be translated to an individual person's entirety and is used in that fashion in Genesis 49:26 and Deuteronomy 33:16. His whole person is gold, pure gold, the best of the best. Hebrews 1:3 (ESV) says, *"He is the radiance of the glory of God and the exact imprint of his nature."* In the Old Testament, gold is significant. In the temple, gold is representative of the glory of God. The ark of the presence itself was overlaid with gold, and Jesus is the manifestation of the ark of the presence. Comparing Him to gold is essentially saying He is the walking, living glory of the ark of the covenant.

CHAPTER 73

His Spirit Flows from His Stare

His eyes are like doves, beside streams of water, bathed in milk and reposed in their setting

(Song of Solomon 5:12 AMP).

When the bride sang, *"His eyes are like doves,"* she was describing the Spirit being inside the eyes of Jesus. This means that all our interactions with the Spirit are being eye to eye with Christ. The bride has taught us that the Spirit is located in the face of the beloved and that the face of the beloved is in the presence of the Spirit. There is no need to divide these two. *Looking to the Lord is where you find the activity and flow of the Spirit, and concentrating on the Spirit is looking into the eyes of Jesus.* How do you look at the Lord? You give your attention to the Holy Spirit.

She then went into further detail, portraying how the Bridegroom's eyes are our means of perceiving the Spirit when she said, *"His eyes are like doves, beside streams of water."* The word *beside* is a masculine noun, meaning from above. It is used to point upward to Heaven and attentiveness to the Lord. How do you find the activity of the Spirit? It is from above the streams of water; in other words, you have to look up to perceive Him. *You find the location of the Spirit in inward upwardness.*

The word *streams* is not streams like you may think. It means a channel, which is a passageway. A channel can be dry, but we know that in this case it is not, because she says it is a stream of water. The living water of Christ passes through this channel, inward upwardness. You detach your eyes from the thing below, look up, and find the channel in which the living water of God flows. *"And he showed me a pure river of water of life, clear as crystal, proceeding from the throne of God and of the Lamb"* (Revelation 22:1 NKJV).

There is a river flowing, and it is called *Christ*. In Ezekiel, wherever the river was, its surroundings became alive. It caused life wherever it flowed. You can inwardly look up and find the stream of the living water that makes you alive, and this is inseparable from the eyes of Jesus, where the Spirit is. How beautiful a Bridegroom!

She continued her description by saying, "[His eyes are] *bathed in milk."* Obviously, to bathe in water is to remove dirt, and bathing in milk calls your attention to something further than mere cleansing. In the Old Testament, the Promised Land is referred to as *"a land flowing with milk and honey"* (Exodus 3:8 NKJV). The milk is pointing us to the type of Christ, who is our Promised Land. *Jesus is the Promised Land who flows with milk and honey.* In the eyes of the Beloved, that glorious, relational perceiving of one another, we have the activity of the Spirit and the apprehension of Christ, God's Promised Land.

When you look into His eyes, you are cleansed in the experience of His person. Have you ever asked for forgiveness of sin but felt like that sin would never leave you? Then, after experiencing the Lord, it felt like that sin would never happen again? There is something about the experience of the Lord that makes what we know real to us. There have been times when I have repeatedly asked the Lord for forgiveness, yet it hasn't become real to my heart. But when I go into an experience with the Lord, He comes and takes the whole issue from me.

The bride finally described her beloved's eyes saying, "[His eyes are] *reposed in their setting."* The word *reposed* means to sit or rest, and *in their setting* means they are in their proper place. In other words, the Spirit is resting in His appointed dwelling place. *When we come to Jesus, rest is inevitable.* Jesus said, "When you come to Me, I will give you rest" (see Matthew 11:28). *Rest belongs to the place of the presence of the Lord.*

CHAPTER 74

Fragrance Pours from His Face

His cheeks are like a bed of balsam, banks of sweet, fragrant herbs...

(Song of Solomon 5:13 AMP).

Balsam is a spice. The word used for *bed* here is a garden bed. His cheeks are a garden of spices. Walter Buettler said, "You can turn airports into a garden of spices with your beloved." The "garden of spices" is the sense of the Lord. His fruit and fragrance are found only in His face or cheeks. It is important to recognize that, to experience the fragrance of His cheeks, you must draw near to Him. You cannot experience the fragrance of His face if you live at a distance. A. B. Simpson said, "These men that yell out to God must live far away from Him." You cannot know such sweetness at a distance.

She described His cheeks as being, "Banks of sweet, fragrant herbs." The word for *banks* is towers or high places. He is in the low garden and in the high tower; He is humility and holiness. He is not only the fragrance that we experience on earth but all the sweetness of Heaven. Jesus said, the *"angels always see the face of My Father who is in heaven"* (Matthew 18:10 NKJV). In drawing near to His cheeks, you see the fruitfulness of the face that the angels know. When we draw near in love, we are living in a way that makes sense to the angels who behold Him.

CHAPTER 75

His Lips Are Medicine for Each Malady

His lips are lilies dripping with drops of myrrh
(Song of Solomon 5:13 NASB).

She described His lips as lilies, similarly to what we read in Job 23:12 (NKJV), *"I have not departed from the commandment of His lips; I have treasured the words of His mouth more than my necessary food."* The word *lips* used in Job is pointing to divine language or God's voice. Lilies were used during this time as medicine, so she was comparing His language to being as medicinal as lilies. In other words, He heals you by speaking to you.[50]

There are times when we have wounds in our hearts and we or others try to bandage them but without success. But *when we are alone with God and hear His voice, He begins to heal us with the tender whispers from His lips.* One word from Jesus can do more than fifty years of earthly counsel.

Lilies are one of the most color-varied plants in nature. The many colors teach us that God speaks in many ways. His voice has such variety that He has medicine for all your maladies. Give more mind to the medicine than your maladies; in other words, stop thinking about your issue and look to the Great Physician of wounded souls.

The bride continued with, *"His lips are lilies dripping with drops of myrrh."*[51] In Exodus 30:23, myrrh is used in the process of making anointing oil for the priests, meaning the anointing comes from His lips. *Your anointing is the sum total of the things that God has said to you.* He makes you what you are by what He speaks to you. *You cannot be anything other than what God has spoken into you.* As He speaks to you, He forms you into what He designed you to be. The anointing is the dripping of the oil of His lips. The anointing of the Spirit is the result of the lips of Jesus. Missionary evangelist Daniel Kolenda said to me one day, "When God kisses a man the fragrance never goes away." His anointing is not sought but caught.

A few verses later in the song, she returned to describing his lips by saying, *"His mouth is full of sweetness"* (Song of Solomon 5:16 NASB). The word *sweetness* is referring to something that you drink. You can drink His words; we drink of the sweetness He has stored up for us. Everything in His mouth is sweet.

Leonard Ravenhill said, "If you have the smile of God, what does it matter if you have the frown of man?" There is nothing better than when you know He is pleased with you by His sweet smile—not only His smile, but also His kiss. When He kisses you, there is a sweet transaction of the soul. He plants kisses on you like seeds, the bloom and blossom of which are the fruit of the Spirit. The more He kisses you, the more you will become like Him. You might say, "Eric, my heart is bitter and harsh." Let Him be your remedy and kiss you with His mouth so full of sweetness.

CHAPTER 76

His Nail-Pierced Palms Uphold All

His hands are rods of gold set with beryl...
(Song of Solomon 5:14 AMP).

She moved from His head to the rest of his body, now describing his hands. The word *hands* in this verse is translated as "strength." God calls His works *"the works of His hands"* (Psalm 111:7 NKJV). In other words, God works in the world through His hands. Jesus said, *"If I cast out demons with the finger of God, surely the kingdom of God has come upon you"* (Luke 11:20 NKJV).

The bride is saying His works are like rods of gold. The word *rods* indicates a "pivot or a hinge on a door."[52] Everything "hinges" upon God's hands. What is the greatest work of God's hands? Is it not the hands that were pierced with nails or the hands that were nailed to the cross? Jesus' death on the cross is the greatest demonstration of what God opens and closes for us. His hands are hinges, demonstrating and executing His strength, glory, and power. This is the beautiful Blood-King. Blood is upon all His gifts. His works are impaled palms.

Her description continued with, "[His hands are] *set with beryl.*" The word *set* is translated to "finished." The work of His hands is finished. Hanging as God's hinge from nails in His hands, He cried, *"It is finished!"* (John 19:30 NKJV).

In Exodus 28:16-20, beryl is one of the gemstones placed on the breastplate of the high priest. He would come before the Lord with these stones upon his chest and intercede for the nation. The stones would glow in the presence of God. The work of the hands of our High Priest is complete.

CHAPTER 77

He Is Altogether Lovely

...And he is wholly desirable...
(Song of Solomon 5:16 NASB).

Finally, our bride proclaimed of her Bridegroom, *"He is wholly desirable."* The word for *wholly* means each, every, all, everything, the whole, the entire. Each of His ways, everything about Him, all His person, everything in Him, the whole of His entire being is desirable. He is attractive, desirable, precious, and everything about Him fulfills everything about you. There is a Man on the throne, and every eye is looking at Him. The angels are moaning with transfixed longing, *"Holy, holy, holy"* (Revelation 4:8 NKJV). There is nothing as beautiful as He. Therefore, nothing could be so desirable or fulfilling as He.

"What is so special about your Beloved?"

There is a charm in His every feature. The One I love is the glory of God, dripping blood, standing out among all others. He is the glory of God, yet restricted Himself to the frailties of a human body and took upon Himself my sins. In His eyes I see the Spirit of God; as I look up to Him, I am refreshed and dipped in Him as God's Promised Land. He is rest itself, and to be near Him is to sense the sweetness of Heaven here on earth. His whispers heal me and anoint me. All things hinge upon the work of His pierced hands, and I am safe under His rule built upon God's throne. He holds me in security and stability with the strength of His legs as He stands higher than all others. His sweet Word is thrilling to my taste, and His presence is the fulfillment of all my desires. He is a friend to me, and the Love of my life. That is what is so special about Him.

CHAPTER 78

The Bridegroom's Chamber

Draw me after you; let us run. The king has brought me into his chambers…

(Song of Solomon 1:4 ESV).

You are the apple of God's eye; you are the treasure of this God of mine. No matter where you are in life, whether you're fantastic or awful, know this: *He is head over heels for you.* He wants to hear your voice. He loves when you turn your attention to Him. Simply doing so makes His heart race. If the inner life is anything, it is a life of being sick with love. Heralds that come forth from the King's chamber as those who have been so deeply touched and intimately kissed drip with God's fragrance. If the gospel is anything, let it be the fragrance of Heaven (see 2 Corinthians 2:15-16).

I write to pluck the strings of your heart. I write not with a hammer to dash you, nor a whip to flog you, but with a honeycomb to exhilarate your heart with the taste of Christ. Oh, that we would taste Him, again and again, as our daily life supply. You may say, "I've already tasted." Then you ought to be the most excited about tasting Him again. I am constantly praying to the Holy Spirit, "Give me the voice of the Bridegroom." This is most important to me when I am preaching or when writing.

One day, I felt the Lord speak to my heart through my nine-year-old daughter while I was playing Barbies with her. She was spontaneously dialoguing between two Barbies. One said to the other, "Girls don't want to be yelled at when they're being proposed to." I thought that it was brilliant! Jesus is always so tender. His voice is like tranquil, passionate love-whispers that break bones (see Proverbs 25:15).

CHAPTER 79

"Open to Me"

…Open to me, my sister, my darling…
(Song of Solomon 5:2 NASB).

I don't think there is a clearer phrase that conveys God's desire for His people to yield to Him than these three words, *"Open to Me."* This may seem elementary, but for Him to say such a thing to us indicates that we are responsible for His entrance. The sad fact is that in one way or another we are always finding ways, directly or indirectly, to shut Him out. What do I mean? I mean that we choose to go on in His things, His language, His power, His purpose, His gifts, His family, and His realm while no longer looking to Him as our source and center. For our Christianity to be "in Christ," everything must emerge from and through the presence of Christ.

Whether intentional or not, many of us live totally unaware of His presence. It never dawns on us that He mourns over our lack of awareness of His presence. *It never even crosses our minds that He is waiting for us, always ready, willing, and longing to be all to us.* We all tend to be easily distracted from Him. I know this about myself; I am forgetful. I am consistently confronted with many issues that stir my self-consciousness, so I get sidetracked and, consequently, my heart becomes hardened from the ease and simplicity of giving Him my attention. I know that if I am to receive Him through communing with Him, I must first be open to Him. And if I am ever to open to Him, it follows from turning my attention to Him.

Oh dear reader, you who have struggled to find the sweet abiding presence of God, if you get quiet and listen, you can hear Him, even now, whispering, "I am here. I am here. Open to Me, My love. Let me in." The omnipresence of the Lord (the fact that He is always with you) shows us that the ultimate sin, self-consciousness, is living moment-to-moment unaware of His presence.

Jesus is looking through the door, reaching His hand through whatever opening there may be, so that we might see Him. He loves for us to perceive Him. He hopes that, if we can even slightly perceive Him as He reaches for us, He might arouse our desire to experience His love in communion with His person and presence. Jesus knocks. Jesus speaks. Jesus reaches, "Give Me your attention. Respond to My presence. Open to Me." Oh, dear reader, who is not yet convinced of our dire need to perceive God, the implanted faculty of our spirit at our new birth is the very means by which He perceptibly communes with us, exchanging love with us, and setting up His rule in our hearts. Jesus is showing us that through this He can become our life-supply.

Even if we do turn our attention to Him, many of us let things stand between us and simply opening the door to let Him in. It is extremely heartbreaking to think of the wounded Son of Man and Lover of our souls "standing behind our wall…looking…peering through the lattice." Julian of Norwich wrote in her book *Revelations,* about a vision of the Lord, "He waits for us…mourning…." He peers through the lattice of our own pride and knowledge—our own "spirituality" and stubbornness—our inattentiveness and arrogance turn us away from His humble person.

Can you hear His whisper seeking to let us know that He is here, longing for us to open to Him? Maybe you don't see the Lord in this way. But the humiliation and suffering on the cross were enough to show His tenderheartedness toward you. *Each drop of blood fell from that cross creating a symphony of His love for you.* As He hung there, His open arms pleaded with all to open to Him. Each day we must remember the openness of the Bridegroom calling to our hearts to open to Him.

I remember I was in a store shopping with my wife, and a song came on over the speakers titled "A Thousand Years" by Christina Perri. The lyric, "I have died every day waiting for you," shot through me like a holy love arrow. I went to the restroom, shut the stall door, and wept. I was touched by His Spirit showing me that the death of Christ daily speaks, "Open to Me. I am waiting for you." Just as He cannot take back His death, He has forever extended the desire of His heart for our hearts to open to Him. The communion elements are a reminder of His waiting and invitation for us to come to Him in all our filthiness. He knows that we are wicked and that we have great difficulty in taking our eyes off ourselves. It is this very weakness that attracts Him to us. We simply need to recognize our deep-seated depravity and cast ourselves upon Him. Even now as you read this book, see Him; hear Him. *The Bridegroom's cross is the certainty of His daily waiting for you.*

You may think that you have shut Him out too many times. You may think that He couldn't possibly still want you in the same way He did the first time He knocked. Oh, dear reader, you misunderstand the way He is. You fail to realize the Bridegroom's tenderheartedness toward His bride. He longs for you. He looks at you. He waits for you. His knock is not restricted, for Jesus says, *"The one who comes to Me I will by no means cast out"* (John 6:37 NKJV).

The invitation goes out to all. The invitation goes out to you. Right now, in the middle of all your issues, in your stress, in your brokenness, there is a divine table that descends from Heaven spread for you, for any, for whoever will yield and let Him in. As Madame Guyon beautifully penned:

Come, ye poor afflicted ones, who groan beneath your load of wretchedness and pain, and you shall find ease and comfort! Come, you sick, to your Physician, and be not fearful of approaching Him because you are filled with diseases; expose them to His view and they shall be healed. Children, draw near to your Father, and He will embrace you in the arms of love! Come, you poor, stray, wandering sheep, return to your Shepherd! Come sinners, to your Savior![53]

Maybe your question is, "How do I open to Him?" or, "What does it even mean to open to Him?" It is encapsulated in a single word *surrender*. Some might use the word *yield*. Let me give an example of the hindrances to surrender or yielding. This may serve as a better description of what it means to yield than even the clearest definition.

Many times, publicly, we begin to sense the moving of the Lord upon our hearts and immediately think, *If I give myself to this, I don't know what is going to happen to me. I am not sure what it will look like. What will people think of me?* Or we say to ourselves, *Why here? Why now? Could we do this later?*

Many times, when we are alone, some of us can sense Him behind the door of our hearts saying, "Open to Me," and we will approach the door by recognizing that He is near, yet we will do everything short of actually letting Him in. We hold ourselves back from Him. We may acknowledge Him. We may press up our ear against the door, but contact will only happen when you cross the point of no return and open to Him. *He will give Himself to those who cast off all reservation and yield themselves to Him.*

Whether in public or in private, we must realize that the disposition of yielding is the same whether you are in a public place or a private place. The sense of His presence is His knocking on the door, but to open to Him, we must yield, and then and only then will He come in.

For some, the resistance is fear; we fear what He will do to us. We are afraid that He may alter us in some way that would rob us of some cherished pleasure or aspect of our personality. For some reason we think He will take something that we love from us. He is not that way. We often fear to give things up to Him out of a fear for their safety. But *nothing is safe that is not committed to Him.*

We must realize that only if He is everything can He safely give us anything. He is the ultimate pleasure, and any cherished thing apart from Him is inferior. God animates your personality. The Spirit enhances every pleasure. But oh, dear reader, if there is something that He must take from you, He takes it to spare you from the deadly effects of an "uncleansed love" and replaces it with the ultimate satisfaction of Himself. He will always lavish Himself upon those who come to Him.

As Tozer said, "Surely God would not have created us to be satisfied with nothing less than His presence if He had intended that we should go on with nothing more than His absence." In the words of Paul the apostle in Romans 8:32 (NKJV), *"He who did not spare His own Son, but delivered Him up for us all, how shall He not with Him also freely give us all things?"*

CHAPTER 80

Lovers Love to Be Alone

My dove in the clefts of the rock, in the hiding places on the mountainside, show me your face, let me heart your voice; for your voice is sweet, and your face is lovely
(Song of Solomon 2:14 NIV).

The enjoyment and bliss of the bride is to live a life of intimate receptivity. In the first chapters of Song of Solomon, the bride says, *"Let Him kiss me"* (Song of Solomon 1:2 NKJV). It is important to note that the bride's disposition is one of yielding, not action. She does not say, "I am gonna kiss Him." As Madame Guyon wrote concerning the experience of God, many times, "Activity obstructs union." With such a surrendered heart, the bride rightly says, *"Let Him kiss me."* The word *let* means permission. *God waits not for the perfection of the life; He waits only for the consent of the heart.* He knows you are powerless to change yourself. He also knows the power of His own kiss upon your life. Therefore, He waits for the consent of the soul, and He will rush in like a love-drunk bridegroom to rescue and thrill our hearts with His kiss.

There is no softer heart than one that lives in the kisses of God. Oh, here is a good place to stop and quietly say, "Jesus, I love You."

This intoxicating love exchange is likened to wine, *"for Your love is better than wine"* (Song of Solomon 1:2 NKJV). Immediately following the kiss, it is written, *"The king has brought me into His chambers"* (Song of Solomon 1:4 NKJV). A kiss, a drink, a love exchange with Him who now pulls you alone into His bedroom! *Solitude is the Lover's chamber, and wine will always be the beverage of the bride.*

So often, people have encounters with God—which is great. They experience a massive outbreak of the Holy Spirit in a meeting, and then a couple weeks later, they return to life as is. This exact tragedy is my burden. Why would such a tragedy occur? It's simple: *The public touch has got to turn into a private kiss—or it will all fade away.* A public touch will happen if you avail yourself to meetings. A private kiss will happen if you avail yourself to Him. That private kiss will solidify your experience and knowing of Jesus and cause what you've gained in God to endure. *The reason He gives a public touch is to draw you to a private kiss.* Oh, the public kiss turns to a private touch, and the bride passes into the realms of glorious, joyful perceptions of Him. Oh, the lovesick know these realities, and their souls salivate for them again and again.

When the infection of lovesickness first entered my being, I didn't know exactly what was happening to me; however, I longed for more. In fact, I had such a deep desire for solitude. Solitude is the chamber of the King. Solitude is a realm in which men can see the invisible and hear the inaudible. Solitude is where man experiences the tangibility, sensibility, and edibility of God. The Shulamite bride craved the same thing. She said, "Meet me in the clefts of the rock in the steep pathway, all alone" (see Song of Solomon 2:14). Lovers love to be alone. They instinctively seek retreat, a retreat in which no other voice is heard, and no other face is seen. A retreat in which the sights and sounds thrill the soul like nothing else. This is what He wants with you. *You must receive the love of God continually so that you can love God back continually.*

The secret of the bridal chamber with God is this: Look to be kissed before you even say anything. Often, our closets are so cluttered with words that we push out His kisses. It's the kiss of God that creates the bride. It's only the kiss that can make us single-eyed. See, the kiss is your cure! The kiss is your call! His kiss can cure your evil and bring you into bliss! The kiss kills so much darkness in the heart of men. You become His lips for mankind by being kissed by His lips. His kiss connects you back to the One for whom you sigh. There is an infection of affection for you!

CHAPTER 81

When Jesus Discloses Himself

The one who has My commandments and keeps them is the one who loves Me; and the one who loves Me will be loved by My Father, and I will love him and disclose Myself to him
(John 14:21 NASB1995).

Do you see what happens when you love Him? You get a disclosure. This word actually means a personal appearance. In other words, "If you love Me, you get personal appearances."[54] There are people who go into their rooms and leave the same way they came in because they never loved. They may have done many things, but never once were their hearts crying, "Jesus, I love You."

This is a problem because God only discloses Himself—literally, shows Himself—to those who love Him. He's made it this way because He is not looking for a warrior or a CrossFit champion. He's looking for a bride who receives her beauty from Him. He returns for the one who loves Him and comes out to meet Him with the oil of love. While the self-disciplined are proud of themselves, the lovers enjoy themselves.

A. W. Tozer said, "Let no man say he wants more of God because if he wanted more of God he would get more of God, because He gives Himself freely to all." So many are not wrapped in the enjoyment of

God because they're tied down by all of the things they want from Him. But in seeing Him, His beauty blinds us to everything else. He is the remedy. He has never been otherwise than all that's fair. Even in the crackle of the flame, the martyrs sang of His infinite charms. Is there not a charm in His every feature?

> In sight of Him
> Rubies turn to toys
> And emeralds sordid dust
> Pride is worthless noise
> And mansions morbid rust.
> —My twist on C.H. Spurgeon's words
> in *The Most Holy Place*

I pray that lovesickness would come upon you. I pray that you'd be brought to a place in where you say, "You are here, Lord, what more could I want?"

CHAPTER 82

Pregnant with Purpose

He called you through our gospel, that you may gain the glory of our Lord Jesus Christ

(2 Thessalonians 2:14 NASB).

If we are to have any authentic relationship with God as we as Christians claim, experience is crucial. *I cannot take experience out of my relationship with God any more than I could reduce my marriage to a photo.* My marriage is highly experiential with sound, touch, voice, presence, work, joy, pleasure, and much more. If I take experience out of my relationship with God, then all I have left is an idea.

In speaking about experiencing the gospel, let me be as candid as I possibly can: Nobody gets pregnant holding hands; it is simply impossible. There must be an intimate encounter and physical transference for conception to ever transpire. Many Christians, if not most, are literally holding hands with Jesus side by side, yet there is very little to no real intimate experience of Him; true reception of His Word in the sweetness of His presence is rare.

So many merely have new lifestyles and new terminology, meet with new friends and listen to different music, struggle with the things that we used to do as heathens and feel badly when we sin. This is all due to a lack of a deeper sense of God in our everyday lives. *I am afraid that too many are content to experience Him only in the public place, but conception only happens in the private place.* If I could speak even more candidly, there are certain things that I will only do with my wife when we are alone. So it is with the heavenly Bridegroom: He will only perform certain things when the door is shut and the heart of His beloved is fixated only on Him.

Many people wonder why they are not pregnant with God's purposes, or why they cannot give birth to those dreams that come from His heart. They are perplexed as to why they cannot overcome sin or see the fruit of the Spirit consistently in their lives. But just as a pregnant woman cannot hide the fact that she has been with a man, union with God cannot be hidden. And no one can reflect a light brighter than what they have actually seen themselves. *We must experience Him ourselves.*

It is important to note that no one gets pregnant reading, *What To Expect When You're Expecting.* Just in case you are not familiar with this book, it is a large volume on the effects of being pregnant. A woman could memorize such an in-depth work, but it will never inseminate her. There are many believers who live this way: They think that, if they memorize and study the Bible, they will somehow find union with God and receive the infusion of His divine substance. It is purely impossible. Man needs to receive God's words through the Scriptures and other means, such as visions and impressions, in the sweetness of His presence alone with Him, where no eye can see.

It should go without saying that no one gets pregnant by telling themselves that they are pregnant. But we have whole movements based upon reminding yourself of who you are in Christ, speaking things into being, or simply "right believing." *Our mental acrobatics cannot perform the miracle of sweet intimacy with Jesus.* It seems that our human mind will come up with anything to substitute a genuine face-to-face love exchange with God in His presence.

No one can get pregnant by desiring a child. Desire alone will never create union or the miracle that results from that union. Let me just add here that having children is not the purpose of intimacy, but the result of intimacy. In the same way, God is intimate with us because He loves us, not so that we would produce offspring. We must consider that the inevitable result of intimacy will be productivity, but it is never the purpose. *Intimacy unites us with Him so that our works issue out of what we are through union with Him.*

If fruitfulness were the purpose of intimacy and not the result of this love union, then God would not be looking for a bride; He would be searching for a surrogate. On the flip side, if man looks to God for power and results alone, then ministry has become a mistress instead of his offspring of love union with His God. Everything in God is all about the mingling brought by the sweet intimate reception of His Word in the bliss of His presence.

No one will become fruitful in this life simply because he or she has a great desire to be. There are whole movements based on "crying out" and fasting and frustrated pleading with God for something to happen. But, dear reader, this is so important for me to pass on to you: *The interactive fellowship with the Spirit is our uniting experience with God, not our desire for it.*

Along the same lines, no one gets pregnant by commitment alone; otherwise, my wife would have become pregnant the moment we said, "I do." God has given us such great parallels in our daily living of the life He wants to share with us, and marriage is a powerful one. But commitment to someone doesn't automatically mean that you are intimate with them. Though commitment is a beginning, it is still possible to be married and not be intimate.

Let me interject here that the reason why so many people know very little about the ecstasies of God is because they have no commitment to Him. Fornication is sin because it is the expression of covenant without covenant. In essence, we are telling God that other things are more important to us than our relationship with Him. *Before God will overshadow you with the blissful intimate experience of His nearness, there must first be a settling in a man's heart that all other loves are refused.* As is stated in marriage ceremonies all over the world, "Forsaking all others, keeping only to thee." God will not pour His Spirit into a man who is not fully His.

Yes, commitment is fundamental, but some people really believe that, because they are willing to die for Christ and His cause, they are becoming like Him. But this is not the case; a man needs the presence of God to unfold the living voice of God into His soul. And those whose lives are truly His will give themselves to experiencing Him every day.

Lastly, no one can become pregnant by knowing the "methods" by which to do so. Without getting too explicit, one can know every way to be intimate and yet not experience intimacy with another person. Just because we can teach about prayer and have learned everything concerning the intimate life, it doesn't mean that we are living by that ecstatic experience ourselves. Experiential union comes from experiential fellowship alone.

We are to come out of the King's chamber, pregnant with God's purposes. We must go forth from the King's chamber to find the lost and invite them to be loved by Him. The great emptiness inside men is that they are missing Him. God's heart was so heavy with love for the lost that it dropped Him to the earth. When sin came in, man had forfeited God in his life, and the great hole in his heart is simply stated, "You are missing from me." God gathers men back to Himself, not by demands, but by a demonstration of love on the cross forever unparalleled.

And so, this is the desire that burns in my heart for the Church: that she would come into a deeper awareness, consciousness, and intimate experience of God's presence in her daily life. There is simply no substitute for it. Experiencing God is not an option. This issue is life and death. A life of experiencing God is authentic salvation. This is the abundant life—the lovesick life.

CHAPTER 83

The Chains of Earthly Passions

Nevertheless I have this against you, that you have left your first love

(Revelation 2:4 NKJV).

Many years ago, my family and I went to the zoo. The eagle exhibit was depressing. These majestic eagles, made for the heights and glories of skies unknown to men, were chained to the ground. I could only see the parallel of people who have lost their first love. Those who are made to live in the heights of first love with God have not only fallen but have become chained to earthly passions. It reminds me of the questions Spurgeon asked regarding the bride of Christ, "What? Thou the spouse of Christ and yet content to live without His company?"

Robert Murray M'Cheyne was writing a letter to an unbeliever, trying to persuade him to love God and to give his life to Him:

> "I have had more joy this morning than you have had in your entire life." After spending time with the Lord this morning, I wrote in my journal, "I feel like I lived a lifetime of bliss in just a few hours." Oh the sweetness of His presence! While others are weighed down by questions and the need to know everything, brides are those who live without a why and join

the minstrels of the skies, and sing the melody of His name, "Jesus our way, Jesus our truth, Jesus our life!"[55]

While the heat of life drains others down, the bride will rest underneath the shadow of His tree and eat His fruit and be refreshed. Her distinguishing mark is this: the presence of the Spirit enjoyed, causing the yielding of fruit. The bride of Christ will testify to the world that a half hour with God will make up for a lifetime of agony and will be faithful through the sufferings of this world. The bride comes forth from the sweet seasons of communion with her invisible God, having received things that no one can take away. In that place, she receives things that we would not give away for 10,000 pieces of gold, land, or even countries. One word from His lips is worth more than a country laid at our feet. May your life be lived in the heights of first love and never come down.

CHAPTER 84

Admitting Our Idols

Do you love Me more than these?

(John 21:15 NKJV)

Jesus wants our love. Our hearts are His prize. I can sense the Lord longing for our highest love. *"Do you love Me more than these?"* Jesus asks us. He has asked me this many times. I travel a lot, and I miss my family. I miss my wife. I love being with my wife, my best friend. My kids weep sometimes when I leave. Sometimes, in service to the Lord and obedience to my call, I miss special things with them that I will never be able to experience again.

At times, my heart hurts, and I want to go home. But when I'm feeling this way, I begin to lose myself in worship. The Lord seems to come to me and show me my daughters. He shows me my wife. I see them like they're in a movie. It almost feels real. And then He whispers in my ear, *"Do you love Me more than these?"* And I have to open my heart and look deep inside and see if I have an idol. When my heart settles and I say, "Yes, I do, Lord. Yes, I do," He takes my heart up into Himself. Highest love reaches the highest places.

> There is One more precious to me
> More precious than family, liberty, heritage or history,
> Someone who's more precious than prosperity and victory

DELIGHTING IN HIS PRESENCE

It is Him who is in me
Lord, there's no light to dim Thee
No effort could ever win Thee
You give Yourself freely
I give my soul to Thee.

—Eric Gilmour

CHAPTER 85

Neglecting the Bridegroom

The watchmen who make the rounds in the city found me,
they struck me and wounded me; the guards of the walls took
my shawl away from me

(Song of Solomon 5:7 NASB).

Have you ever felt the effects of neglect? Madame Guyon wrote in her journal, "By neglect I have been pillaged." To be pillaged is to be overtaken and robbed unnecessarily. We find, when we neglect the Lord, we get into all sorts of unnecessaries. The bride was struck and wounded with unnecessary scars. Her shawl was also taken. Neglect brings unnecessary losses. The bride then realized in neglect that her safety was in the beloved's person.

I feel as though the Lord looks at many of His people and asks, "Did you marry Me, or did you marry him? Did you marry Me, or did you marry that?" It doesn't matter what "that" is. It could be a person or a pursuit, yet if it has more of your attention than Jesus, it will negatively affect everything.

Is not our lack of peace and joy an indication that our love is somewhere compromised? Perhaps a person in your life has more of your attention than Christ. Let me ask you, did that person die for you?

Maybe an interest has risen up and captivated your heart more than Christ. Did that interest rise from the dead? Most certainly not. Yet our Bridegroom bled, died, and rose to win first place in your heart.

We should never let a day go by that we do not drink deeply of Him. The holy Bridegroom has given His limitless Self as an installed well of Living Water. There is no reason to be dry because you have God inside. The bride should be the most satisfied person the world has ever seen because she has a Bridegroom. In essence, Jesus asked the woman at the well in John 4:5-24, "Where is your husband?" She responded, "I do not have a husband." And Jesus said, "That is your problem."

You may say, "I have all of these problems in my life." Your problem is that you do not have a husband. You need to marry Jesus. The woman had five husbands. That is indicative of searching the world for something that only Jesus can be. Only Jesus can satisfy the soul.

That is Bridegroom-Living-Water Christianity. He will lift you above earth and wrap you in His bliss. Charles Spurgeon said, "Since the road to Heaven is Heavenly and the road to bliss is bliss, who will not follow Jesus? My soul be thou in love with the way as well as the end, as Jesus is one as well as the other."

CHAPTER 86

The Danger of Additions

One thing I have asked from the Lord, that I shall seek: that I may dwell in the house of the Lord all the days of my life, to behold the beauty of the Lord and to meditate in His temple (Psalm 27:4 NASB).

Do you see what David was saying here? He was saying that his one singular desire was looking at God. *The definition of prayer is sustaining the sweet sense of His person.* That's it. It's lingering, attentiveness to Him. It's far more important that He have all your attention than that you know what to do. *We often want to know what to do when what He wants is you!* He wants your heart, affection, and attention.

Throughout the Bible, the only person who ever used the phrase *"one thing"* like this was David. I find it interesting that the only person that God ever asked, "What is the one thing that you want?" was David's son, Solomon (see 2 Chronicles 1:7). It was almost as if the Lord were saying to Solomon, "Could your heart be anything like your father's?"

After David had passed, God had no one crying out, "One thing!" So, God approached David's offspring in pursuit of such a heart, and Solomon asked for wisdom. Wisdom is a good thing, and Solomon's answer pleased the Lord, yet it still was not the highest thing. Why? Because it didn't keep Solomon until the end. In fact, the Bible says,

"Solomon loved the Lord...except..." (1 Kings 3:3 NKJV). Often, we love the Lord, yet there is an exception—a *but* on the end of our sentence. Or we say, "I love You, Lord, and...." Did you catch that? *It's the excepts and ands and buts added to our love that kill us. The additions are deadly.* They are literally toxic. If the Christian walk is getting difficult, it's because we've added things to the equation that were never intended by God.

As wonderful as church atmospheres are, there is potential for us to latch on to so many other things. Yet there is power in our willingness to get simple. The simplicity of Jesus can cure us of the complexities of charismatic culture. Praise God for an appetite for spiritual things, but they all must come secondary to the person of Jesus. Perhaps you're like an eagle on the ground. You've woken up, shaken off sleep, straightened out your feathers—but you haven't begun to ascend into the altitude you're called to dwell in. I encourage you to fly up above in the place where only One exists—Jesus. That place is higher than gifts, higher than anointing, and higher than prayers. It's bridal union with the person of Jesus! His face is available for you in unlimited measure. *He is inexhaustible as a person.*

I want to lift Jesus high, as He is the only way to altitude; in fact, He is the altitude. So often, we get so heavy, burdened, and bogged down with stuff. It's easy to look *in* God's direction and not look *at* God. *We can get mesmerized with His things and forget Him.* For example, I could be looking in my wife's direction, be listening to her, yet not have eye-to-eye contact with her.

I remember looking at my wife in the kitchen one day, and I wanted her attention. She was doing motherly things. I grabbed her and said, "Give me your attention."

She said, "I've got all of these things to do."

I took her and grabbed her by the chin and looked her in the eyes and said, "I love you." A couple nights later I was awakened in the middle of the night by someone grabbing my chin, yet nobody was there. It was Jesus. He grabbed my chin because He wanted to lift my chin up to look directly at Him. Often our head is down, and He lifts our head, because we cannot see Him when our head is down.

Oh, friend, you are the apple of God's eye. If you could see how much joy you bring to His heart, you wouldn't even believe it. To believe this and remind yourself of this is very, very important. Let me tell you something about God: He is jealous for you. *He will not share you or your attention with anything else.* In fact, sometimes He hides the future from you on purpose. Why? He wants to make sure that He has all your attention. He wants you to be caught up with Him, not where you're going or even the purposes He has for you. *He won't share your attention with your future.* He would rather end all His purposes through you than to lose your heart's affection. You might have prayed over and over, "Lord, show me what's to come. Show me where I'm going." *Your desire for guidance has supplanted your desire for Him.* Sometimes He blocks your view of all these things you need, to give you the only true thing you need—Him. *He is more interested in feeding you than leading you.* Hudson Taylor said, "Many love Him truly, but not love Him only." Let our love be only for Him and not Him and all the additions. In this, you'll wake up in the morning, and your first thought is, *I want to be with You, Lord.*

CHAPTER 87

Seeking Our Own

[Love] *does not seek its own...*

(1 Corinthians 13:5 NKJV).

When I first was born again, I used to go into my room and long to be filled with God. I would read Pentecostal preacher Smith Wigglesworth's story and how he would sing, "Filled with God, filled with God, emptied of self and filled with God." A desire to be possessed and filled would overtake me in a way that my body could not handle. Something would break in me every time. It had to be broken again and again. What was this? Self-will. Our self-will begins to mend over time, so it must be broken again and again. As humans, we are in love with ourselves, and this is what hinders our loving the King, our Bridegroom.

The apostle Paul wrote, love *"does not seek its own."* The bride does not seek her own. If we seek our own, we are not bridal. If we seek our own interests above Him, how is that bridal love? That would be acting as though we are not married while we are married. In one sense, it's a kind of breaking covenant with Him or, at the very least, despising covenant with Him. When we live a life that declares, "I'm going to do what I want to do," we are testifying to the Lord that we don't want to belong to Him. Remember the two become one. This means *your wants and desires are to be lost in Him, for Him.* As a result, you have the heavenly joy of receiving Him as everything you need.

He knows you better than you know you. He can give you the things you really want that you don't know you really want. You think you know what you want. But you don't really know you because you didn't make you. He crafted your entire internal make-up and knows just what will satisfy you. God will sometimes withhold what we think we want because He knows that which we want would indeed make us miserable should we obtain it. The Maker knows best. It is best if we stop trying to force things we think are what we want and simply yield to Him.

CHAPTER 88

"Will You Go with This Man?"

Then they called Rebekah and said to her, "Will you go with this man?" And she said, "I will go"

(Genesis 24:58 NKJV).

Remember in Genesis, Abraham, the father of the faith, wanted to find a bride for his son. So he sent out his servant to find this bride. Now follow carefully. Abraham is a shadow of God the Father, looking for a bride for Jesus Christ. God has sent the Holy Spirit into the world to find the one who will marry His Son.

The servant found Rebekah, and when he saw her, he began to give her gifts from the bridegroom. Yes, he gave her gifts, but his ultimate intention and purpose was to take her to the bridegroom. This is exactly what the Spirit of God is doing now. He comes and gives gifts to point you to the Bridegroom. He wants to grab you and take you to the Bridegroom Himself—namely, Jesus! If we stop short of the Man, we miserably miss everything. He wants to meet with you, marry you, and numb you to doubt, unbelief, fear, and all the things that scatter your soul. It is a sad fact to note that many Christians have received the gifts and said, "Thank You for these gifts," and all the while have no intention to go on to the Bridegroom. It's so easy to cheat on God with stuff

He gives us. Literally, the gold in their hands has outshined the One who sent it as an indication of His beauty.

Now here is the crisis (turning point) moment. *"Then they called Rebekah and said to her, 'Will you go with this man?' And she said, 'I will go'"* (Genesis 24:58 NKJV). In that moment, she had to decide to leave behind the provisions she had always known and from this moment on find her provisions in her bridegroom. The question before her meant forsaking all she had known to find all she would know in him. Her response was everything. She said, *"I will go."*

The Holy Spirit may have healed your heart, blessed your life, given you guidance when you needed it, yet now the question is being posed to you, "Will you go with this Man? Will you give first place and total trust to Him? Forsaking all others will you keep only to Him?

Are you willing to say goodbye to everything else to find everything in Jesus? In the same way Rebecca began to find her provision, satisfaction, fulfillment, and protection in her husband, so we are to find everything in Him. We can no longer find these things in others or ourselves. If we marry Jesus and still try to satisfy ourselves, we sabotage the whole thing. If we marry Jesus and still look for other people to fulfill us, satisfy us, protect us, or keep us, we sabotage the entire marriage. Marriage means, "Only You Forever."

When I feel temptation at times in my life, I'll say that to the Lord, "How can I give my heart to another when You have taken my heart from me?" Or I will say, "Here is my heart. Take it from me. It is safer with You than with me."

Refusing to sin is far inferior to refusing to depart. God has not brought us into a life that merely says no to sin. He has brought us into a life in the Spirit in which the Bridegroom is blissfully enjoyed, and we remain with Him. *If you experience Him as He desires you to experience Him, your longings and cravings will be so satisfied that you'll look nowhere else.* You'll be able to say with the psalmist, *"The Lord is my Shepherd, I shall not want"* (Psalm 23:1 NKJV). My wants are gone, vanished in the sight of You.

CHAPTER 89

Jesus, Our First Love

I know your deeds and your toil and perseverance, and that you cannot tolerate evil men, and you put to the test those who call themselves apostles, and they are not, and you found them to be false; and you have perseverance and have endured for My name's sake, and have not grown weary. But I have this against you, that you have left your first love. Therefore remember from where you have fallen, and repent and do the deeds you did at first...

(Revelation 2:2-5 NASB1995).

When we look at Christ's words to Ephesus in Revelation 2, we see that Jesus was speaking to a people who understood that He wanted them to want Him. They could be identified as those who hold the revelation of *"the great mystery."* Ephesus was likely the only church in Revelation to which Paul wrote an epistle.[56] And in the book of Ephesians, Paul spoke of *"the great mystery"* —a phrase that is only used in writings to this church. What is that great mystery? Paul said the great mystery is the fact that a man leaving his father and mother to be joined to his wife is *"concerning Christ and the church"* (Ephesians 5:32 NKJV). It's a bridal mystery! A mystery of love. Speaking of love to the Ephesian church would make sense to those who already knew of this mystery of love.

We see that there are positive things in this message. Jesus said that He knew their toil. The word *toil* means that they persevered amid pain.

There are so many Christians who live their lives persevering even when things get difficult. Jesus commended this. He also noted that they didn't quit. They're like Marines taking the beachhead.

In addition, they had a zero tolerance toward evil. They had a love for righteousness, and they didn't mess around with sin. They tested those who call themselves apostles.[57] Not only this but they hadn't grown weary. All these things are good and commendable.

Yet the uppercut Jesus gave should get all our attention. They had left their first love. This should show us that *toil is inferior to love. Perseverance is inferior to loving Him.* Even being able to discern who is true and who is false in doctrine is inferior to loving Jesus. Avoiding evil is inferior to loving Jesus. You can stay away from evil, have clean doctrine, persevere in pain—yet if you fail to love Him in your heart, you are breaking the great mystery that the Ephesians were taught so well. Jesus essentially was saying, "You are doing great, but you don't love Me anymore." Those who understood the bride and Bridegroom relationship had regressed and no longer loved Him like they once did.

Even when we have so many things that appear outwardly right, correct, and in order—we can still be inwardly fallen. We think that fallen is defined by someone committing some sort of immorality, yet Jesus thinks of having fallen in a different way. It's when He no longer has first place in the heart and when the mornings are not designated for Him who will illuminate the entire day. *When He is no longer the one who is kissed, loved, and adored, you have fallen.*

Jesus didn't say, "You lost your first love." He said, "You left." This word *left* in the Greek is the word *aphiémi*, which means to send someone away. They had much going right, yet they had sent the Lord away. As a dear friend of mine likes to say, "They dismissed Him."

They continued in their doctrine, duties, and disciplines, but the Lord was gone. This word *aphiémi* is also used for divorce, which is in keeping with the phraseology of the great mystery. Furthermore, it means to neglect or no longer keep. Jesus was conveying that they had kept all these other things yet let Him go. Their hearts were given to other things for Him, yet not given to Him.

The one word of His exhortation I want to draw you to is simply *remember*. *"Remember therefore from where you have fallen..."* (Revelation 2:5 NKJV). Sometimes in my life, just one simple remembrance of His love toward me is the spark to light the flame of my love again. When I begin to feel estranged from Him in my heart or have not kept in sweet love exchange with Him, just one memory can come in and melt my heart. *He masters our wills by melting our hearts.*[58]

I don't know where you are in your life, but perhaps this is exactly what the Lord is saying to you. Perhaps you've kept on when it was difficult, and you've even avoided sinning against Him. But your heart is far away.

Maybe your doctrine is sound, and you understand the Bible fully. Yet Jesus is saying, "Remember our love exchange? Remember your head upon My chest? Remember our tears together?" Christ's definition of falling is not adultery, pornography, embezzlement, or something of a criminal offense. His definition of falling is this: You don't love Him with all your heart.

You ask, "Eric, what does it mean to have first love?" Personally, I have heard many definitions. I like all of them. First love is not merely a place but a person, namely Jesus, and can be written in capital letters—FIRST LOVE. First love is when He comes first above all other things. First love is the love you had for Him at first. No matter which definition you use, they all capture the heart of the matter which is that Jesus wants your love and your heart.

"Do the deeds you did at first" is an interesting command. What were those deeds He was referring to? To answer that, let's look at a quote from British evangelist and Bible teacher G. Campbell Morgan, "Zeal for the Master that is not the outcome of first love is worthless." What are the deeds we should return to? The deeds that are issued from first love. Robert E. Murray famously added, "No amount of activity in the King's service will ever make up for the neglect of the King."

He wants you. You can give Him all sorts of stuff. Some give Him their hands, "I'll do all of these things for you." Some give Him their minds, "I'll give myself to theology." Some give the Lord their feet, "I'll go where you want me to go." Yet all this is inferior to you giving Him your heart. His message to Ephesus is clear: Give Him your heart. If you've grown stale in the Lord, this can be a call from Him to remember your first love. Remember what it was like to live in the heights with Him. Do those things you did at first. Let everything that you do issue out from the sweetness of His presence.

CHAPTER 90

The Jealousy of the Bridegroom

Set me as a seal upon your heart, as a seal upon your arm; for love is strong as death, jealousy as cruel as the grave. Its flames are flames of fire, a most vehement flame

(Song of Solomon 8:6 NKJV).

The jealousy of the Bridegroom burns like a flame and flashes like fire. Do you remember when you were first born again and you were so deeply in love with God and nothing would challenge Him? In fact, you were offended when someone suggested that they could take God's place in any way. Nothing would keep you from spending time with Him. You saw everything that stood between you and your prayer closet as a devil from hell. I'm telling you such a love shapes your value system.

Do you remember when hours felt like minutes? Do you remember when the entire Bible seemed to breathe? Do you remember when the sound of worship caused an eruption inside you? The mere thought of being able to worship together with people was sheer joy. Do you remember when there was such an ease in His presence? There were difficulties and tribulations around, no doubt, but for some reason you just soared above them. These were the heights of first love.

Do you remember the sensitivity to the Spirit in the beginning? Do you remember the internal ache in your heart for God? Do you remember making meals for your family and weeping while you did? Washing dishes with dish soap and tears? Do you remember having to pull over while you drove to cry before the Lord?

God remembers these things. He longs for your return. He tells His people throughout Scripture, "Remember!" His message is the same today. First love is what makes the heart of God so happy because in it He gets exactly what He wants, which is to captivate your heart. His goal was never to corner men and collect their consent, but to captivate men's hearts.

Many want to take repentance out of the gospel, yet Jesus says, "Repent," to those who are saved. (See Revelation 2:5,16,22; 3:3,19.) When you take repentance out of your life, you burn the bridge that leads back to first love. In one of his many sermons and writings, Charles Spurgeon wrote:

> See the secret of strength, look at Jesus and overcome. Let us lament our infrequent use of this conquering weapon. Now for a long and loving look at the Bridegroom of our hearts. Help us Holy Spirit, to whom we owe our sight.

See, the eyes of the One whom you love masters you. To live in the consciousness of His presence is first love. The secret to overcoming is being overcome by Him.

> Tell me you're in the ocean, and I'll walk into the sea; raise the waves of Your love, and I'll let them bury me. —Tyler Gnott Gregson

CHAPTER 91

Reminded of His Kindness

But the Helper, the Holy Spirit, whom the Father will send in My name, He will teach you all things, and bring to your remembrance all things that I said to you
                                              (John 14:26 NKJV).

If you know anything about Jesus and have walked with Him for any period of time, you know that He is distinctly romantic. God has a way of sweeping us away to experience sights, sounds, and smells of His presence and character. Suddenly, we find ourselves reminded of His sweetness and longing for more of Him.

When I was in the Brownsville Revival, they used a very distinct air freshener in the church. Up until that point, I had never experienced that smell before, and for years and years after, I never experienced it again, until recently.

I went into an Italian restaurant, and as soon as I walked into the restroom, I smelled the same exact air freshener from years ago at Brownsville! I immediately fell to my knees and said, "I remember, Lord! I will not forget what You did for me. I won't forget how You kissed me. I'll live for you all of my days wholeheartedly."

It's as if the Lord brings these things back up just to remind us of our affection for Him and His affection for us. How gracious and compassionate is the Lord! He reminds us of these moments when we, through the craze of life, start to forget them. We all have, unintentionally, at one time or another, forgotten these romantic yearnings for God. He comes leaping over the mountains to remind us again and again. *He loves for us to relive how He saved us.* It keeps the flame of our hearts lit. And oh, how He loves to save us, again and again. He doesn't save us once and then never saves us again. He wants to save us daily. Not that you are born again over and over again, but it sure does feel like it. Life enters in, and love ignites in us day in and day out.

Sometimes when we start to become numb to the things of God (unconscious of His presence), we will hear His voice. It could be through a song, a book, a smell, or a word. The Lord will place something before you to remind you of His love for you. He doesn't stop at speaking; He even knocks. If you knock on a barrel, you can tell if it is empty or full. Sometimes the Lord will do the same with you. He may knock to show you the condition of your heart. He may do this by using someone or something to challenge you.

Even in the times of our distraction He is so kind. In Song of Solomon, the groom is searching for the bride and peering through the windows. He didn't look through one window (singular) and say, "Oh, she isn't home." He went to every window, determined to find her. This is our Lover. He looks for you. Seeks for you. Longs for you. The entire Bible is God longing to have His people all to Himself, for us to find Him is all we will ever need. Oh! What great love He has for you!

How many times has God broken your heart with kindness? Does not His gentleness break a bone (see Proverbs 25:15)? I read that one of the Puritans said, "If He would just strike me for my sins, I wouldn't feel so bad about them." What was he saying? When you are in Christ and you are growing in Him, He sees you as perfect and is always there to uplift you and encourage you. *He is not here to whip you; He is here to woo you.*

CHAPTER 92

He Keeps Us

The Lord keeps all who love Him
                    (Psalm 145:20 NASB1995).

That's the essence of what marriage with Christ is. We love His presence and His words. I don't understand people who say things like, "What's more important? The Bible or the presence?" When somebody asked Charles Spurgeon this question, he replied, "What's more important? Breathing in or breathing out?" We love Him and His voice. We love His voice and Him.

It's simple and so straightforward—a child will understand it. Sometimes people want to put an asterisk there, as if to say, "The Lord keeps all who love Him, but...." You can't add a disclaimer. The language is clear as day. *"The Lord keeps all who love Him."* This means that our job is not to keep ourselves. *Our job is to love Him.* And when we give more of our time to keeping than loving, it's no wonder we're not kept. You don't need to keep yourself. You love Him, and He will keep you. That's the key.

CHAPTER 93

Joyfully Taken

For your Maker is your husband, the Lord of hosts is His name; and your Redeemer is the Holy One of Israel; He is called the God of the whole earth

(Isaiah 54:5 NKJV).

Dear reader, you are the bride of Christ. This is who you are. You are taken with the Groom. When others are excited over things "interesting" and "new," you will be one of those who are dazzled by the beauty of the Bridegroom. A safer haven I cannot find than loving Jesus above all others. This is fruit that remains. As His bride, we will not dishonor our Bridegroom by being joyless in His presence. We will not dishonor our Bridegroom by giving a greater eye to our own garment. We will not dishonor our Bridegroom by giving the attention that He deserves to things far inferior to Him. We refuse to do these things because we are those who are captivated by His love.

We who live in communion with God, experience joys in Him that are far beyond comparison to the things of this world. All earthly joys are like the earth: earthy. *But the joy of Christ is like Christ: heavenly.* All the things that flow from Him are of such a higher quality than the earth. We are those who live on the highest quality of existence. This is what makes us different from everybody else, not only because it makes us happier than everybody else, but because He transforms the way we live our lives.

MARRY ME

In conclusion, Jesus looks at you and says this:

Marry Me, let Me be all to thee.
None can be what I can be.
Give ears to hear and eyes to see.
Fill your soul with ecstasy
and fill your heart with joy and peace.
Make eternal wars cease
and lift you above life's miseries.
Take you into My victories
and love you now and endlessly.
Marry you eternally,
present Me as one sent to you, mocked and rent for you.
Blood spent for you.
Death sentence to cross, shame, and grave,
oh let Me save you again.
Only I can mend through the Spirit I send,
so come to Me and be one with Me.
Give your soul, and you will behold and know My Father.
Are there any others with affection greater than mothers
and deeper than lovers?
I will smother your sins away and cover you with My pinions
and lay at My chest with a quieted rest.
I'll end all of your quests, stilled and caressed.
I am the best for you.
Victory through making you new
by a love you have never known,
by a substance I alone am.
For I am the Son of Man.
Turn your heart to Him.

—Eric Gilmour

CHAPTER 94

Simeon, a Listening Life

And behold, there was a man in Jerusalem whose name was Simeon, and this man was just and devout, waiting for the Consolation of Israel, and the Holy Spirit was upon him
(Luke 2:25 NKJV).

Simeon means "listening" or "to listen." If you think about what listening is in its most basic understanding, it is simply *attentiveness.* And if you think about what attentiveness is, it is the exclusion of all other things except the thing you are focusing on.

So, *Simeon* means giving God all your attention at the exclusion of all other things. It's living a life of listening. Simeon lived his entire life waiting for the coming of the Lord. It is this waiting, listening, and the exclusion of all other things that is the heart of what I want to continue to emphasize.

The Scriptures say specifically that Simeon was *waiting.* But it says firstly that the Holy Spirit was *upon him.* Secondly, it was *revealed to him* by the Holy Spirit that he would not see death before he had seen the Lord's Christ, and thirdly that he *came in the Spirit* to the temple.

There are three things that will accompany a life that listens to the Lord and is literally attentive to Him at the exclusion of all other things:

1. The Holy Spirit will rest upon your life.
2. The Holy Spirit will reveal. You will have revelation from the Spirit, spiritual thoughts, spiritual words, spiritual unveilings that lead to the revelation or are the revelation of Jesus.
3. Your life will be quickened and moved by the Spirit.

The Holy Spirit resting on your life, the revelation that comes from the Holy Spirit, and the Holy Spirit's movement or empowerment, all come from listening. When living a life that gives God all your attention, the Holy Spirit can rest upon you, move you, and reveal Jesus to you.

I believe *Simeon* is what God wants to say to you right now. And I pray that God would grant you grace to listen, to live listening, attentive to His sweet presence. And as you're attentive to His presence, during even the mundane and all the busyness of life, living listening is living in attentiveness to God.

Many times, it is the addition of other things in our hearts that cause the entrance of fear, anxiety, competition, comparison, and condemnation. All these things that come into the human soul and make a man have to fight and wrestle on the inside are normally leaked in through *inattentiveness*.

I want to encourage you that *listening* is what God is after. This is what will help you. It will place the direct contact of the Spirit upon you. I love the word *upon* because it suggests *underneath*. It suggests that something or someone is over you. It is subjection to God's presence. We cannot claim to be subject to God's presence if our hearts are not attentive to His person. We are attentive to the person of God in being attentive to the presence. And we are attentive to the presence in being attentive to His person.

So, I encourage you that this is yours; it is the New Covenant. No matter what's in front of you, no matter what life situation you are in, you can live listening.

CHAPTER 95

The Sound of His Voice

His voice was like the sound of many waters
(Revelation 1:15 NASB).

Did you know the "voice" or "of many waters" in Revelation has to do with peace being communicated to you? As a matter of fact, just recently Pennsylvania State University studied the effects of sound on the human brain, and in their findings, they realized that the human brain files sounds away into two different categories: threatening or non-threatening. You have sounds that are threatening, causing an alarm inside, and then you have sounds that are non-threatening to you. Included in the sounds that are non-threatening is the sound of running water, flowing water, or the sound of water itself.

The researcher from University of Pennsylvania wrote that the sound of water on the human brain is not merely non-threatening, but it's actually calming. The study even went on to say—now these are their words, not mine—that it's as if the flowing of many waters is saying, *"Do not worry, do not worry."*[59]

I share that to say, when we hear the sweet sound of God's voice, it dispels doubts, fear, and unbelief. He brings in the sweet quiet of His own person. Inside His voice is such a peace and freedom from the restless worries and the anxieties of life, for His voice is like many waters. He quiets the heart with His love. He comes in and causes the peace that passes all understanding to spread throughout your whole being. Such peace is not only a wonderful experience to live under, but it also is told to us to guard our hearts and minds (see Philippians 4:7).

There is a story about several men working in an icehouse. Before modern refrigeration, there were barns where they stored ice and covered it with hay, keeping the room cool to serve as a refrigerator to preserve foods. Several men were working in an icehouse, and while they were working, one of the men lost his watch. When they came out of the barn from working all day, the man said, "Oh, I lost my watch in there." So all the men went into the barn, and they rummaged through all the hay and moved the ice to look for the man's watch. All their efforts proved to be fruitless.

When they came out, the man was saying, "I can't believe I lost my watch." A little boy standing nearby heard that he couldn't find his watch and that he had lost it inside the barn. So he went into the barn and within ten minutes, came back with the watch. When he returned the watch, the man looked at the boy and said, "How in the world did you find this? We all rummaged through the hay, we moved the ice, and we searched every piece of straw. How did you find my watch?"

The little boy said, "Well, I went into the barn, and I shut the door, and then I lay still and quiet until I heard the ticking of the watch."

I share that to say, for many people, their prayer life is rummaging through the straw, moving the ice, trying to gather many people together to try to affect some sort of encounter with God. But here is the truth—if you will go into the closet and shut the door and silence your heart before Him so that He has all your attention, you will hear the sweet ticking and find the great treasure, the lost treasure, of the person of Jesus. *You will find the riches of the Lord right there in the secret place within.*

I encourage you to take some time today to be like that little boy with the watch. Go into a room and be quiet. Lay your head upon His chest and lift your heart up to Him. Let Him know how much you love Him and receive His love for you. Your heart will begin to open up, and then as you open up the Scriptures, they will open your spirit even more. There are three openings: (1) You open your heart to Him; (2) He opens you up; and then (3) the Scriptures open more for you to receive more of Him. These are three realms: (1) I open one, which is my heart; (2) and then His love opens another; which causes (3) the Scriptures to open me to His person. Open to open to open to receive revelation upon revelation upon revelation of Him.

CHAPTER 96

Becoming His Image

And we all, with unveiled face, beholding the glory of the Lord, are being transformed into the same image from one degree of glory to another. For this comes from the Lord who is the Spirit
(2 Corinthians 3:18 ESV).

When I was a young boy, my dad used to say to me, "I can see myself in your eyes." He'd look at me closely when he said it. The Lord brought it up to me one day and said it to me as my heavenly Father, "I can see Myself in your eyes." With my own daughter, I looked at her and said the same thing. Then, she looked to the left. When she did, it dawned on me, I could no longer see myself in her eyes. I could only see myself in her eyes when she looked at me. *God will only see Himself in you when you look at Him.* If something else takes your attention away from Him, He won't see His character in you anymore.

The other day I was in prayer, but I was all over the place. Perhaps you can relate. I was there, I was praying, yet I wasn't really looking at Him. I finally said, "What am I doing?" I stopped, looked up, and just said, "I worship You!" I felt like the Lord said, "There you are." You can teach it yet forget it: *Adoration is the key to seeing.*

There is a day coming in which God will contrast your image with the image of His Son (see Romans 8:29). This coming Judgment Day will not be a day to take a written exam to test your knowledge, nor a day to look over your résumé of service.

I remember a story that changed my view of the judgment seat of Christ forever. A dear preacher woke up in the middle of the night in a cold sweat, having had a dream in which he saw the judgment seat. As he drew near to the throne, and closer to his moment of accountability, he began to rehearse in his mind the things that he had accomplished for God while on the earth and prepared the tip of his tongue with his résumé of service. Just before he was able to release such a self-application before God, God said to him, "Come closer. I want to see how much of my Son I can see inside of you."[60]

It is not about how much we can do for God, but rather, God for us on the cross, God in us by the Spirit, God out of us as His works, and God's reward to us at the Judgment. No other quality of works will survive the test of fire (see Romans 11:36; 1 Corinthians 3).

CHAPTER 97

Abandoning Self-Consciousness

And when I saw Him, I fell at His feet as dead. But He laid His right hand on me, saying to me, "Do not be afraid; I am the First and the Last"

(Revelation 1:17 NKJV).

Abandon your need to understand. Let His presence be more to you than answers and explanations. Whatever our hesitation is to opening ourselves to the presence of the Lord, it originates in an unwillingness to forfeit self-consciousness. Let me give an example through a story.

Earlier this year, I was at a conference in Houston, Texas, where I was called to introduce a dear friend. I had been unable to stop crying during worship because of a deep sense of God's presence. Noticing this, the host of the night said to me, "Before you introduce our brother, let them know what has been happening to you." As soon as I started to speak, I could feel an intensification of the presence of the Bridegroom. At first, I was wondering what the Lord was doing, while also trying not to reveal that there was such an overwhelming sense of God inside me. I thought to myself, *What if I am the only one who feels this right now? What if I give in to this, and I look like a total fool because of the timing and lack of "spiritual atmosphere" among the people right now? After all, I am supposed to introduce another.*

At that moment, I blurted out, "If you will yield to Him in the way that He is moving on you, He will be able to come into that area and perform a deep work in your heart. But on the contrary, if you do not yield to Him, He cannot perform that work." I said, "You have to forget about yourself and everyone else. To yield is to say with all your heart, 'I do not care what other people think or what happens to me. Come in, Lord, and do whatever You want to do to me.'" The moment those words came out of my mouth, the Lord placed a question before me. "Even if they do not open to Me, will you?"

I saw Him with the vision of my soul, standing at the door of my own heart, asking me to value Him more than my appearance before respected men and woman of God. "Open to Me," He whispered. I froze. As I vacillated between yielding and not yielding, three seconds felt like three hours. And with the simplicity of giving up, I caved in at His feet and broke down to a sobbing mess. Once I inwardly threw off all restraint, pride, and self-consciousness, a rush of love hit my whole being like a tidal wave, and I began to cry from so deep within that I felt I would vomit. Currents of God flooded my body over and over. People began to come from all over the meeting and get on their faces before God and weep. Needless to say, God performed a deep work in my heart that night. I still feel the effects of it to this day.

It is important to note that, had I not yielded, surrendered, and opened to Him, it would have altered much more than just that night. I would be different today. Not to say that another opportunity would never have come, but because I yielded and looked like a complete fool in front of thousands. Such an abandonment released me to be more His than I otherwise would have been had I kept the door closed and been content to merely hear, but not respond, to the voice of His invitation to a holy love exchange.

Even as you read this now, I beg you on behalf of the Lord, do not be content just to sense the invitation. Don't be content merely to hear the knocking of His holy hand upon the door of your heart. Yield; open to Him. He is your loving Bridegroom.

Abandon all other things and turn the gaze of your soul upon Him. Once you sense the slightest impression from His Spirit, cast off all restraint and cast yourself upon Him in absolute trust. Let Him take you, whether you are in a service, a meeting, the kitchen, or in your closet. These impressions are a heightened sense of awareness of His person through which you may pass into Him and Him into you. It is a union, an entrance into one another, a moment that carries your heart into fresh perceptions of Him. Most often, these sweet precious impressions will happen to you in times of waiting in His presence. But if they take place anywhere else, or at any other time, there is a reason. Let me encourage you, above all, do not resist Him, for stubbornness deteriorates our hearts. Stubbornness is a resolute adherence to one's will.

Yielding is laying your will at His feet, the resolute adherence to His will. Dear reader, yielding to the sweet impressions of the Spirit is the best way to cherish God Himself. Cherishing Him is the greatest stewardship of Him. The greatest saints are not those who have fasted the most, or those who know the most, or those who are loudest or most entertaining, but rather, those who have learned the beautiful depth of attentiveness and surrender to God.

CHAPTER 98

My First Vision of the Lord

…Have you seen him whom my soul loves?
(Song of Solomon 3:3 ESV)

The first time I ever saw the Lord I tried my best to write in my journal a description of what I saw, heard, and felt. I combine all three because I am not sure which one it actually was. He was unadulterated sensory overload. My words, pen, and paper were merely a feeble attempt to explain our soul's magnetic attraction to God.

I wrote, "Upon what seemed like seeing Him, in that very instant every one of my desires were pulled toward Him. I was stricken breathless by the overwhelming conviction that He was unlike anything I have ever seen before. The only thing that I could say through my tears and groaning was, 'I do not want to live (here) anymore. Take me with You.'

For me it was the ultimate Maranatha experience. The Spirit in the bride truly aches for His return (see Revelation 22:17). Let me put this in perspective. I have a beautiful wife and two lovely daughters. My family and life are blessed, and I am deeply thankful for these naturally unparalleled joys in this life. But I want to explain that the vision of Him was so magnetic that I wanted to forfeit all of it and everything in this life, forever, to simply always have Him in this capacity. Now, I know that is not at all He wants from us, and I apologize for the weakness of words, but I must at least attempt to convey the meaning of how beautiful and enjoyable He is. He is the gravitational pull to our being.

If you pick up a rock and drop it, it is pulled toward the ground. So it is with the soul and the magnetic force toward God. He will pull it to Himself entirely. The only reason our soul will not come to Him is tolerated obstructions. If you pick up the same rock and drop it to the ground with a table under it, it will not hit the ground but stop at the obstruction of the table. Idols and inordinate affections act as that tolerated obstruction to our vision of God and our pull toward Him. This is why John, who described God as light and fellowship with God as walking in the Light, wrote, *"Little children, keep yourselves from idols"* (1 John 5:21 NKJV). We need to guard our hearts from anything that would take God's place in our hearts.

When we see the magnetic pull of God's glorious beauty, we can understand why it is written, *"Rightly do they love you"* (Song of Solomon 1:4 NKJV). In other words, "I have seen You, and I totally understand how You can capture someone's heart with one glimpse." He who has seen says, "All should love you. It is right to do so." When we truly see His beauty, we recognize that it is wrong not to desire Him. It is the ultimate sin, for He is the ultimate beauty. In fact, *all sin is a gaze away from Him.* Idolatry is placing something in front of your gaze upon Him. It is a fixation upon a beauty that is far inferior to Him.

Oh, dear reader, why write such things? I write them because God wants you to know that His affections are for you. The exhilarating love of God is yours to have, to experience, and to live by. His attractiveness is the antidote to this world's glitter and our personal selfishness. To see Him and hear Him, to sense Him and be with Him, is the inebriating bliss of life, the fruit of which is real life-giving holiness. Holy living is the unobstructed Holy One. This is why He died, to give Himself to you.

CHAPTER 99

"She Loved Me"

Assuredly, I say to you, wherever this gospel is preached in the whole world, what this woman has done will also be told as a memorial to her

(Matthew 26:13 NKJV).

Here was a woman who had poured out her *"costly fragrant oil"* from *"an alabaster flask"* and upon the head of Jesus (Matthew 26:7 NKJV). Her name was Mary of Bethany, and Jesus wanted her to be *remembered*. If that's true, then she must be significant! Not only that, He tied the memory of her to the global spread of the gospel.

At first this bothered me, because I thought to myself, She never preached a message. She never taught a class. She never wrote a book. She never performed any miracles. She is only mentioned three times in Scripture. I said, "Lord, what could it be in this woman that would cause her to be tied to the testimony of Your name for all time? What is it that's so special to You?"

As I waited, I heard His voice. He said, *"She loved Me."* It doesn't sound significant, does it? I thought, *Lord, so many people have loved You! What makes her different?* I realized that God took me to this passage to show me the *kind of love* that she had, which separated her from so many others. The kind of love that she had was intrinsic to the spread of the gospel.

CHAPTER 100

Seated at His Feet

Now it happened as they went that He entered a certain village; and a certain woman named Martha welcomed Him into her house. And she had a sister called Mary, who also sat at Jesus' feet and heard His word

(Luke 10:38-39 NKJV).

The first mention of this woman Mary describes her as sitting at the feet of Jesus. Think of this picture: a crowded house full of commotion, and then there was this woman. She was on her knees, and with fixed eyes, she was steadily staring at Him. If I had been there, I would have been struck by her magnificent obsession. It would have hit me hard. Why? Because she didn't care what anyone thought of her. She was looking at Him. This is the life I want! To gaze upon the Lamb who was slain.

Mary teaches us something very significant. She teaches us that He is too beautiful to look away from. She teaches us that there is honey dripping from His lips (see Proverbs 24:14). That honey which drips from His lips is sweet to our taste! Consistent with this, the psalmist wrote, *"How sweet are Your words to my taste, sweeter than honey to my mouth!"* (Psalm 119:103 NKJV). With the mouth men can describe honey, but only the mouth of Jesus dispenses honey. The difference is that teaching and theology will always be inferior to tasting. Proverbs also states, *"My son, eat honey because it is good, and the honeycomb which is sweet to your taste; so shall the knowledge of wisdom be to your soul..."* (Proverbs 24:13-14 NKJV).

I see that the story of Mary of Bethany is a call to be captivated by Him! She is a demonstration of His worth. She is a proclamation of the preeminence of His person. Her love cries out, "He is greater than His gifts! He is more wonderful than His wonders! Stare at Him for He is greater than the anointing. He is lovely!" She wasn't standing in awe of His powers. She had found something so much more valuable. She found that He Himself was the fulfillment of her soul, the satisfaction and joy of her life. She was struck breathless by the overwhelming conviction that He is more lovely than anything she had seen.

Mary of Bethany realized that being with Him was to have everything she had ever wanted, it was to be everything she had ever wanted to be, and it was to arrive everywhere she had ever dreamed of going. She found that His presence freed her from the need to have anything else. Most of all, she found that her prayers had vanished simply by His presence.

How? Because she found that He was and is everything she needed and everything she ever wanted. His presence transformed the mundane and common house that she lived in into a garden of spices with her Beloved. She drew near, near enough to hear, if nothing else, His breathing.

CHAPTER 101

One Thing Is Necessary

But one thing is needed, and Mary has chosen that good part, which will not be taken away from her
(Luke 10:42 NKJV).

Many may think, "I don't know this life." Let me tell you, Jesus described this life as *"that good part."* He went on to describe it as untouchable and eternal! Following that, He said, *"One thing is needed."* In other words, "The only necessity in life is right here. It's looking at Me."

Mary shows us that the essential Christian message is not to behave, but to *behold*. You can tell who doesn't really want God to rule their lives by who doesn't take time simply to sit and listen to Him.

I wake up at times and put my head on the headboard and just say, "Lord, I have to see You. I have to see You. I worship You. I must see You." The sweetness of God begins to flow in as the receptivity of my soul begins to open through adoration. He flows in with great peace. He fills my heart with joy. I tell you that these things are for us! In this, all the situations in our lives have no bearing on whether we have peace and joy. Why? Because we are mesmerized and fixed on His person! This is what Mary was trying to show us.

CHAPTER 102

The Barrenness of a Busy Life

But Martha was distracted with much serving, and she approached Him and said, "Lord, do You not care that my sister has left me to serve alone? Therefore tell her to help me"
(Luke 10:40 NKJV).

Martha was too busy for the bliss and enjoyment of life with Jesus. Her relationship with Jesus was too wrapped up in what she was doing for Him. Oh, how easy it is to hide behind activity! Jesus sharply contrasted the two sisters, Martha and Mary. One was looking at Him; the other was not. One was listening to Him; the other was not. One was near Him; the other was not. One was at rest; the other was not. Martha was simply too active to give Him her attention. The Greek philosopher Socrates said, "Beware the barrenness of a busy life."

Christian author and speaker Martha Kilpatrick wrote in her book *Adoration: Mary of Bethany—the Untold Story,* "Activity can mask an empty soul and give a fake costume of nobility." *Martha chose occupation for the Lord over preoccupation with the Lord.* She wanted to feed Him more than feed on Him. She preferred to be around Him over looking at Him. So many have become fixated on what is around Him rather than fixated on looking upon Him! It's a trap to get us to become mesmerized by His ways rather than His person.

It's so easy to love the flow and forget His face. Oh, but there is a face that can always be looked at! As we continue to look at His face, we become blinded to the things that are constantly pulling on us. This is called *satisfaction*. Satisfaction is not a perk of His presence. *Satisfaction is the very means by which He frees you and empowers you to be able to obey Him.*

Martha was unable to see the real significance of having the Lord in her house. That is exactly what activity can do. It will rob you of your attraction to God. Martha chose to value other things rather than look into His eyes. Martha was fruitless in this scene. The Spirit of God thought that her work was so insignificant that it wasn't even named specifically in the Scriptures. Her work died with her. Yet Mary became a message to all generations connected to the gospel itself. Do you see now?

You ask, "What do I do, Eric? Quit my job and move to a cave? I have twelve kids, I'm in school, and I'm running two businesses." Allow me to define busyness to you. Busyness is not having a lot to do. Here is the definition of barren busyness: *It is to eclipse His worth with work.* It is to replace the simplicity of Christ with the multiplicity of your own ways.

Busyness is not having a lot to do. Jesus had a lot to do, yet it never made its way into Him. He remained disconnected from busyness inwardly to remain connected with His heavenly Father amid everything. In this, His Father became the Source of everything. *Only if He is center can He be Source.* If He is not center, He is not Source; and if He is not Source, something else is. That was Martha's problem.

What is dead activity? It's covering the restless, bankrupt state of your soul with things to do, things that God didn't commission. It's easy to keep outward things going while neglecting the simple act of staring into His face.

Isn't it funny that Martha tried to diminish what Mary was doing? But notice that Mary, just like the Lamb she was beholding, offered no rebuttal! *Workers always try to murder worshippers in one way or another, but to gaze at Jesus exposes the ones who are not gazing.* This shows me that Mary scandalizes all those who love the work of the Lord more than the Lord of the work. It shows me that the purity of only wanting Him exposes the impurity of merely wanting something from Him.

This choice is ever and always before you and me. We are today what we chose yesterday. We are not today what we neglected yesterday. We will be tomorrow what we elect today. The choice is yours. He has made His face completely and totally available.

CHAPTER 103

The One for Whom Jesus Looks

She...called Mary her sister, saying, "The Teacher has come and is calling for you." As soon as she heard that, she arose quickly and came to Him. ...Then, when Mary came where Jesus was, and saw Him, she fell down at His feet...
(John 11:28-29,32 NKJV).

Mary's brother had died. Then the Lord arrived at the scene, and Martha met Him. What did she meet Him with? She talked to Him and gave Him dialogue. Her dialogue was even theological, talking about resurrection and so forth. However, in Christ's dialogue with Martha, He didn't find what He was looking for. So the Scripture says, *"And when she had said these things, she went her way and secretly called Mary her sister, saying 'The Teacher has come and is calling for you'"* (John 11:28 NKJV).

Words will never replace worship. He wasn't looking for someone who would throw words at Him. He wanted worship rather than words. He went looking for Mary! The first time I read this, it pierced me deeply. He sought a worshipper. He still does! He is looking for a "Mary" in the middle of a room. He is looking, not for mere words, but for worship in the middle of every meeting.

Here in the story, Mary came to Jesus. Her brother had died. Her heart was hurting, and she didn't understand. What did she do? She threw herself at His feet. Can you see why she was so special to Him? Everyone else was standing up and talking. They had opinions about this and that, and plenty of unanswered questions. Yet what did Mary do? She threw everything and herself at His feet. An act that professed, "You, Lord, are more lovely and worthy to me than all the answers and facts that I could find!"

Here is the problem: We would rather explain than adore. We would rather inquire than simply adore. Mary shows us that she was willing to worship Him despite not understanding. Certainly, she had feelings and thoughts and questions about the situation—yet she was willing to throw them down, along with her own life, at the feet of Jesus. She was literally saying that *Christ's presence is more important than answers.*

I don't know what you're going through or what you've been through, but I know that He Himself is better than any answer He could give you. Too often, we get distracted by what He gives, and we begin to come to Him for something other than Him. Then we wonder why we keep missing the sweet, blissful enjoyment of His person.

Even though Mary and Martha had similar discussions with Jesus, He responded with resurrection power to Mary only. Do you see this? Mary shows us that *she would rather move Him than understand Him.* She was more interested in touching Him than defining Him. She shows us that something takes place in adoration that makes understanding not that important anymore. The memory of her, which is intrinsic to the gospel, is God's invitation for all to love Him as she loved Him. She is the embodiment of the first commandment.

Mary was mesmerized. In fact, she had symptoms of lovesickness. The primary symptom is a fixed gaze that cannot look away or be broken. I pray that you would become so lovesick that you would have this same problem. In this, what other people do to you or against you, it matters not, because you'd have to take your eyes off Him to see them anyway—and you can't.

CHAPTER 104

Joy to the World

Gracious words are a honeycomb, sweet to the soul and healing to the bones

(Proverbs 16:24 NIV).

God wants to give you a gift. Of course, He wants to give many; but allow me to dial in this teaching on a specific gift. As I do, remember something about a gift: It has nothing to do with you. In other words, all you must do is receive. Your merit doesn't release it; His goodness does. There are no hoops to jump through or special requirements. Red tape isn't the language of the Kingdom.

To be specific, I feel that the Lord is releasing the gift of joy on the body of Christ because it's so desperately needed. We have a serious joy famine on our hands. May this work in some way help to remedy that. Many people deal with a real sense of heaviness. They become scattered in their minds. Excess thinking becomes normal. These things ought not be.

If there is one thing that I'm seeing in my travels, it's this—the Church is lacking joy. The Bible says, *"The kingdom of God is not eating and drinking, but righteousness and peace and joy in the Holy Spirit"* (Romans 14:17 NKJV). Joy is in the Kingdom! College professor and Bible expositor Gordon D. Fee, in his book *Paul, the Spirit, and the People of God*, writes, "Joy is the hallmark of genuine spirituality."

In other words, if there is really a flow from the vine to the branch, the fruit that will come out is a result is joy. You can bank on joy when you touch God. God brings His realm with Him when He comes. His nature is joy. When He is allowed in, He dispenses His person into you. In this, joy becomes part of you, and it's no longer dependent upon circumstances around you, but the God who is in you.

In this mode of receiving, your joy can't be touched by anything in the natural, for your joy is rooted in the vine. I want to tell you, a lack of joy is a lack of life! I was on Anna Maria Island, and the Lord told me something very interesting. He said, "I'm going to change everything about you."

I got away by myself and entered a small prayer chapel to give my attention to Him. I became quiet and still before the Lord. *Quietness is the absence of external noise. Stillness is the absence of internal noise.* As I sat in quietness and stillness in the chapel, I felt the Lord speak something to me. Out of the blue, I saw in a flash the R&B group called 112. I remembered them and thought, *Whoa, the Lord must be saying something to me.*

I instantly remembered Joel 1:12 (NIV): *"... The people's joy is withered away."* I've found that the majority of Christians whom my wife and I know have no joy whatsoever. They may have lots of "revelation," but no joy. They might have a big ministry, and they might have it together on the outside, but they totally lack genuine joy on the inside.

Andrew Murray said, "If the hands on the clock are not ticking, you know there is an internal problem." Likewise, if joy is not present in the life of a believer, you know there is an internal problem. Obviously, there is an attack in this area in the body of Christ. The attack isn't necessarily on joy itself, but it's an attack on our connection to the vine. The evidence of your connection being attacked is a lack of joy. Your joy levels can be used as a measuring stick for your connection with Jesus.

Let me just clear the air. God wants you to be happy! All my life, I've heard different things than that. I've heard that God is not interested in my happiness. I've now learned that He wants me to be so happy, not in stuff and things, but in Him. He wants me to be happy in my reality! So often, people are caught placing their happiness in un-reality.

"*When He, the Spirit of truth, has come...* " (John 16:13 NKJV). The translation for the word *truth* in this passage is the word *reality* in the original text. "When He, the Spirit of reality, comes...." He shows us what is real and what is not real. So many can't decide what's real and what's fake. The Holy Spirit enables us to decipher the difference.

What is real to God? It's the thing that lasts forever! What's real to Him is that which comes from Him, lasts forever, and never began. That is reality to God. The Spirit of reality has come to show you what is real, what came from God, what lasts forever, and what has no beginning. He came to show us the eternality of God, if you will.

It doesn't get any more real than the fact that *a connection to the joyful vine cannot produce anything but a joyful branch*. Our beings haven't come into distant contact with a joyful King, but have literally been infused with His joyful Spirit. This isn't just demeanor-altering truth, but nature-altering reality.

CHAPTER 105

The Best Present Is Always Presence

But now I come to You, and these things I speak in the world, that they may have My joy fulfilled in themselves

(John 17:13 NKJV).

Joy isn't a mere possession, but a person. God instills happiness in us when He offers us gifts. Don't ever allow yourself to be condemned for enjoying that which the Lord has provided. Paul said that God *"gives us richly all things to enjoy"* (1 Timothy 6:17 NKJV). And God has given you His actual person, the greatest riches that we could obtain. When people want something more than what's already here, they cut off their ability to be happy.

I was once walking with my wife in heavy rain, and I said to her, "Babe, I know where a pavilion is!"

She said to me plainly, "Great. Then take me there." In other words, the knowledge of the pavilion being there was not the same as running under it (see Proverbs 18:10). She wanted to be removed from under the influence and oppression of the rain.

In the same way, knowing that Jesus is joy is not the same as drinking Him. Knowing that He is drinkable isn't the same as drinking Him. You can't hide behind theology or anything else. You must simply approach

Him. *Without your heart laid at His feet, something will always try to take His seat.* Jesus won't share His throne with a theology or a doctrine. He wants to sit there personally and not just theologically.

When in prayer, I simply cease my thinking and allow my heart to go up to Him in worship. I begin to drink of the Lord. He Himself said, *"If anyone is thirsty, let him come to Me and drink"* (John 7:37 NKJV). He isn't offering something apart from Himself. He Himself is in the cup. We drink of His own person. Folks wonder how to drink of Him in prayer. It's simple: less thinking, more drinking. What stops us from drinking deep is often thinking deep. We focus so much on what this person says or what that person thinks, and it hinders us from simply drinking of the Lord fully. It's time to not give a rip about the opinions of those around us, but simply place the chalice of God to our lips and allow Him in. Our minds are what hinder us from receiving in prayer more than we might realize. You can drink of Him in public, in private, on the job, or anywhere else. The surroundings are irrelevant when He shows up.

CHAPTER 106

Happy Holiness

And his delight shall be in the fear of the Lord...

(Isaiah 11:3 ESV).

So many people have unnecessary problems going on in their lives because there is something of themselves that they won't replace with Him. As a result, they're unfulfilled and unhappy. Yet Jesus makes us happy.

I have said to the Lord, "You make me so happy!" It's a happiness that cannot be put into words. It's *"unspeakable and full of glory"* (1 Peter 1:8 KJV). The biggest hindrance to this wonderfully happy love exchange is not being willing to lose yourself in Him. One man said, "God is more concerned with your holiness than your happiness." But I have never seen a holy man that is unhappy. *There is nothing more joyful than living a holy life, wholly His.*

The fear of the Lord opens up a happiness within us. It's actually the key. Many are so confused about what the fear of the Lord is. The fear of the Lord is best understood by examining the first time it's mentioned in the Bible.[61] It's in Genesis 22 when Abraham took Isaac onto the mountain to sacrifice him. Everything was in place and ready. Abraham lifted his knife to kill his only son when God stopped the process. What did God say to Abraham? *"For now I know that you fear God since you have not withheld your son, your only son, from Me"* (Genesis 22:12 NKJV). Abraham didn't allow even the most precious and promised thing to take the place of God. I pray that God would expose the things that have taken His place and revive our gaze upon His face.

May we get back to hitting the bull's-eye, which is intimacy with Him. In this, we will experience the sap that drips from His person and walk in the life He has ordained with joy unspeakable and full of glory! A lack of the fear of the Lord has absolutely robbed our joy. The fear of the Lord yields a return called *joy*. You might say, "Well, because I am unhappy, are you saying I don't fear God?" No! What I am saying is that in any area where you've let something block your gaze on the Lord, it is blocking the fear of the Lord.

When the fear of the Lord is blocked, you can't find true happiness. The fear of the Lord is a posture that decrees, "Lord, You are number one! You are the only thing that matters. You are all I need." This fear of God isn't a trivial power play on the part of God, but a means by which He can shed abroad the blessing of joy on His people. Let this be your mainstay and your default.

CHAPTER 107

Jesus Paints Smiles

Therefore God, Your God, has anointed You with the oil of gladness more than Your companions

(Hebrews 1:9 NKJV).

I was once in the closet drinking of Him, and as I did, I slipped into a vision. In the vision, Jesus had a massive paintbrush dripping with red paint. He was dragging it behind Him and walking toward me. I was looking at Him, unsure of what He was about to do to me. Suddenly, He took this massive paintbrush and smeared it across my face and painted a big smile on my face. He then grabbed me and brought me face to face with Him and said, "Happily enjoy all the details of your life!" This changed me forever!

Jesus wants to anoint us with the oil of gladness! He wants to put upon you the oil of joy so that, through face-to-face contact with Him, you can enjoy every aspect of your life. I can hear people saying, "Eric, you don't understand, such and such just happened."

I understand that things happen but use your situation as another window to pass into God and enjoy Him. Paul was so convinced of this evidence of the Spirit that he told the Thessalonians that joy is our way of life (see 1 Thessalonians 5:16).

You might think, *Well, Eric, there are a lot of aspects of my life that are not enjoyable.* That might be true; however, He is with you in them all and thereby provides joy through them all. The Scripture says, *"Therefore*

God, your God, has anointed You with the oil of gladness above Your companions" (Hebrews 1:9 NKJV). In other words, there wasn't another man as joyful as Jesus.

Some might say, "Well, sure, but that was for Jesus, not us." Then we must look at another Scripture in which Jesus says, *"These things I have spoken to you, that My joy may remain in you, and that your joy may be made full"* (John 15:11 NKJV). The joy of Jesus is sharable.

Maybe people speak falsely about you, try to frame you, or say bad things about you. I'm telling you that when God's words have captivated your heart, they are sweeter than honey. There's something about the sweetness of the honey that comes from His lips that takes away all the bitterness that comes from other people's lips. Just listen to Him. Hear Him.

"You have put gladness in my heart" (Psalm 4:7 NKJV). See, God places joy within us. It's His heart in us. Martin Luther wrote, "I know how easily one can forfeit the joy of the gospel." It's quite easy to forget how joyful this life really is. We've failed to remember that, in everything, we can experience joy unspeakable by drinking of Him. I don't share these things to tickle ears or to give a shallow encouragement. I share the message of joy with a deep-rooted conviction that *God is going to break joy open over us in a much-needed way*. It will change everything about our lives! Joy isn't just an idea, but an actual, tangible fruit of God's Spirit.

"In your presence is fullness of joy" (Psalm 16:11 NKJV). What does *"fullness of joy"* mean? It means there is no area that isn't touched with joy. Mother Teresa said, "One filled with joy preaches without preaching." I think often we disqualify ourselves when we try to preach the joyful good news of glad tidings without being touched by joy. How can we preach glad tidings when we ourselves are not glad? When you as a person are dipped into the fullness of God's joy, you will attract people. Folks will want to listen to what you have to say simply because you're smiling so much. If Jesus really did die for us and if He really did set us free, then an eruption of internal joy can be the only by-product.

"Restore to me the joy of Your salvation" (Psalm 51:12 NKJV). In other words, the salvation that you have has joy sewn into it. You separate yourselves from the wonderful victories of salvation when you cease drinking of the joy that is Himself. Are you being convinced yet of the happy intention of God?

108

Glistening Faces

And wine which makes man's heart glad, so that he may make his face glisten with oil

(Psalm 104:15 NASB1995).

In the Scriptures, wine and joy are mixed together. God literally gives wine, which is representative of His Spirit, as a gift. What is the result of drinking of His Spirit? Gladness of heart! Yet it doesn't stop there. He gives reason for this gift: *"so that he may make his face glisten with oil."* What does it mean to glisten with oil? It's the Spirit of God coming out of your countenance. It's displaying the person of the Lord. It's bearing His image.

As these things happen and take shape in our lives, we can preach without preaching. Of course, we should continue to preach the gospel verbally, without question. However, with joy on our countenance, there is a preaching that happens in passing someone on the street. Your spouse needs to see a face that's glistening with oil in their lives. Your children need to look up to mom and dad and see faces glistening with oil. Your friends need a friend to look to with a face glistening with oil. This glistening will only happen through joy in the heart that comes from drinking of the Lord.

The intoxication of God causes such joy. It's for you today, it's for you later, and it's for you always. I'm simply reminding you of things that you already know. It's not just "A holly jolly Christmas," but a holly jolly life! In Isaiah 9:3 (NIV), we see that Jesus increases joy, *"You have...increased their joy."* Oh, how the Church needs an increase of joy. I need it. You need it. Jesus alone can give it.

English author Richard Rolle wrote about this joy in no uncertain terms, "I feel I will die in the face of your joy." Have you ever seen anyone write this way before? He is saying, "I am so joyful that I feel I am going to die." Saint Catherine of Siena wrote, "I am so filled with joy I am surprised that my soul stays in my body." I am writing to tell you that joy is for you. It is God's will that you be animated with joy in His presence.

The presence of God in the person of the Holy Spirit will banish mourning and depression. He will lift the oppression and break the heaviness off your life and replace it with a lifted heart of joy. Oh, your heart may be hurting. You may feel damaged inside because of something you have done or something someone has done to you. You feel pain inside from weariness and dryness. *God does not heal the heart by theology. He heals it by wine. He heals it by the honey of His words.*

When the new wine of Heaven enters, the old religious wineskins burst. May all the weights fall off your life as you enter the joy of His presence. May your home be filled with joy. May your marriage be filled with joy. May your relationships be filled with joy, joy of such a kind that even on your way to be martyred, your heart will sing of His unfailing love and beauty.

CHAPTER 109

Union—A Final Exhortation

That they all may be one, as You, Father, are in Me, and I in You; that they also may be one in Us, that the world may believe that You sent Me

(John 17:21 NKJV).

God has granted to us His own person. I think, at times, this overwhelms us. We begin to think of communion with God or prayer as our religious responsibility, and we say, "Oh, I have to pray today." This is tiring. Only our value of the person of Jesus can quicken our value for communion with Him. *We devalue communion when we devalue the Lord.* But when in the gospel we see His wonderful majesty and that His face is resplendent with glory and that He is the highest delight known to man, then we are drawn into the bliss of fellowship.

Prayer is not, "I have to make sure that I'm healthy. Let me grit my teeth and barrel through communion with God." It's not this way. He actually is inviting me behind closed doors to drink of a wine that is not from this world. He is inviting me to lay down upon His chest and feel His heart beating into my ear and charming my soul into alignment with His person. He is inviting me to be with Him, to walk in the midst of the garden of God and eat from the tree of life. I'm telling you, this is what needs to be revived in our hearts every single day. That is what the gospel of Christ does. We have been invited into the chambers of the King, to enjoy the sweet kisses of God.

All these things that I'm writing to you, you may very well know. But I pray that the Holy Spirit would again quicken you—that the Holy Spirit would again make the gospel real to you. I pray that Jesus would be beautiful again to you and that you would see that this is the most wonderful thing in the world: *to be able to commune with the Man who is above all men.* He is the Man who has been raised from the dead, the firstborn among many brethren, who sits at the right hand of the throne of God, whose face is resplendent with glory, who made John absolutely powerless by just exposing the glory rays from His face to him.

I pray that, today, you would "Turn your eyes upon Jesus, look full in His wonderful face, and the things of earth will grow strangely dim, in the light of His glory and grace."[62] I pray that your heart would be erupting in loving communion with Him. I pray that there would be such an ease and a simplicity that would come upon you, and that God Himself would remove burdens off your shoulders.

Even right now, in Jesus' name, I pray that burdens would come off your shoulders—burdens that you have picked up and didn't even know you had picked them up, but I pray that God would take them off you.

Notes

1. A. W. Tozer, *The Pursuit of God* (Chicago: Moody Publishers, 2015), 96.

2. Reverend Andrew A. Bonar, *The Life and Remains, Letters, Lectures, and Poems of the Rev. Robert Murray McCheyne, Minister of Saint Peter's Church*, Dundee (New York: Robert Carter & Brothers, 1849), 157.

3. This quotation is from Chapter 10 of John van Ruysbroeck's *The Little Book of Enlightenment.* Julie Marks, "Mysticism: John Ruysbroeck—The Little Book of Enlightenment," *The Value of Sparrows* (blog), October 4, 2017, https://thevalueofsparrows.wordpress.com/2017/10/04/mysticism-john-ruysbroeck-the-little-book-of-enlightenment/.

4. Jeff Hubing, PhD, the president of FIRE school of Ministry in Chicago, has spoken about the hyper-grace movement and distorted identity issues in the Church. He has said, "We've become so positional that it is no longer personal."

5. John Brand, "Robert Chapman: Apostle of Love," *Evangelical Times,* July 31, 2012; https://www.evangelical-times.org/robert-chapman-apostle-of-love/; accessed February 29, 2024.

6. Robert C. Chapman, Plymouth Brethren Writings; https://plymouthbrethren.org/author/99; accessed February 29, 2024.

7. John Wesley, *An Extract of the Life of the Late Rev. David Brainerd, Missionary to the Indians* (Penryn: W. Cock, 1815).

8. Richard Baxter, *The Practical Works of Richard Baxter, Vol. 1* (London: George Virture, 1838).

9. A. W. Tozer, *God's Pursuit of Man*, 26.

10. Madame Guyon, *A Short Method of Prayer & Other Writings* (Peabody, MA: Hendrickson Publishers, Inc., 2005), 8.

11. Richard Baxter, *The Practical Works of Richard Baxter, Vol. 1* (London: George Virture, 1838), 24.

12. William Law, *A Serious Call to a Devout and Holy Life* (Boston: T. Bedlington, 1821), 174.

13. Charles H. Spurgeon, *Smooth Stones Taken from Ancient Brooks Being a Collection of Sentences, Illustrations and Quaint Sayings, from the Works of...T. Brooks* (London: W. H. Collingridge, Brooks, 1859), 248.

14. James Moffatt, *The Golden Book of John Owen* (London: Hodder and Stoughton, 1904), 218.

15. Dane Ortlund, *Gentle and Lowly: The Heart of Christ for Sinners and Sufferers* (Wheaton, IL: Crossway, 2020), 23.

16. Charles H. Spurgeon, *Illustrations and Mediations; or, Flowers from a Puritan's Garden* (New York: Funk & Wagnalls, 1883), 237.

17. Charles H. Spurgeon, "Justification by Faith," Sermon No. 3392, The Spurgeon Archive, http://www.romans45.org/spurgeon/sermons/3392.htm/; accessed March 2, 2024.

18. F. B. Meyer, *Our Daily Homily*, Vol. 2, *I Samuel–Job* (New York: Fleming H. Revell Company, 1898), 145.

19. Charles H. Spurgeon, *Spurgeon's Sermon Notes* (Peabody, MA: Hendrickson Publishing Marketing, LLC, 1997), 31.

20. Art Katz Ministries; http://artkatzministries.org/category/articles/; accessed February 29, 2024.

21. "Sermons & Devotionals by Walter Beuttler"; BiblePortal .com;https://bibleportal.com/sermons/author/Walter-Beuttler; accessed February 29, 2024.

22. Andrew Murray, *The Practice of God's Presence* (New Kensington, PA: Whitaker House, 2000).

23. Thomas Merton, *An Invitation to the Contemplative Life* (Ijamsville, MD: The Word Among Us Press, 2006), 92.

24. Jeanne Guyon, *Experiencing the Depths of Jesus Christ* (Peabody, MA: Christian Books Publishing House, 1981).

25. George Muller, *Soul Nourishment First*, A Booklet by George Muller, May 9, 1841, GeorgeMuller.org; https://www.george muller.org/devotional/soul-nourishment-first; accessed February 29, 2024.

26. Jeanne Guyon, *Madame Guyon: A Short and Easy Method of Prayer* (2007).

27. Witness Lee, *The Tree of Life* (Anaheim, CA: Living Stream Ministry, 1987).

28. Witness Lee, *Practical Lessons on the Experience of Life* (Anaheim, CA: Living Stream Ministry, 2001), Chapter 13; http://www.ministrysamples.org/excerpts/THE-WORD-BEING-GOD-HIMSELF-AS-OUR-FOOD.HTML; accessed February 29, 2024.

29. Lyle Dorsett, *A Passion for God: The Spiritual Journey of A. W. Tozer;* A.W. Tozer & Wheaton College, February 27, 2012; https://recollections.wheaton.edu/2012/02/a-w-tozer-wheaton -college/; accessed February 29, 2024.

30. Arthur Bennett, ed., *The Valley of Vision: A Collection of Puritan Prayers & Devotions* (Eternal Life Ministries).

31. The Lamb alone is found worthy to open God's scroll and look into it (see Revelation 5:4-5). And so it is with any and all revelations of Christ that proceed from the Scriptures.

32. Andrew Murray, *The State of the Church* (Ada, MI: Bethany House Publishers).

33. Charles Spurgeon writes, "Why do people try to paint this lily and gild this refined gold? The gospel is perfect in all its parts and perfect as a whole: it is a crime to add to it, treason to alter it, and a felony to take from it." *The Treasury of David: Spurgeon's Classic Work on the Psalms.*

34. A. W. Tozer, *The Pursuit of God.*

35. Charles Spurgeon, Sermon #2899, 7/9/1876; https://www .thegospelcoalition.org/blogs/justin-taylor/preach-christ-or -go-home-and-other-classic-spurgeon-quotes-on-christless -preaching/; accessed March 1, 2024.

36. Art Katz, audio sermon from sermonindex.com.

37. See Psalm 25:1; 121:1; 123:1.

38. Acts 1:1 teaches—*"the thing Jesus began to do and to teach"*— that Jesus does not merely "practice what He preaches," He preaches what He practices.

39. Cure De Ars wrote, "Prayer is God looking at me and me looking at God."

40. When Moses was to share the burden on his life with others in Numbers 11, the Scriptures show us Moses knew the men that he chose; he chose them based on that knowledge; he brought them away into the tent of meeting; God came to Moses in

front of them; and God made the transfer. Moses' communion with God was the means by which he manifested God to them. Moses was a type of Him who was to come. Jesus is the One Moses spoke of (see John 5:46). Moses prophesied Jesus would be his fulfillment (see Deuteronomy 18:15). Jesus is greater than Moses (see Hebrews 3:3).

41. John Wesley, *New Testament Commentary* (Grand Rapids, MI: Baker House Publishing, 1957).

42. Craig Keener, *The IVP Bible Background Commentary* (Madison, WI: Intervarsity Press, 1993).

43. Romans 8:9,11,13-14,16; Galatians 5:22.

44. See John 17, Matthew Henry Commentary; https://www.biblestudytools.com/commentaries/matthew-henry-complete/john/17.html; accessed March 1, 2024.

45. Saint Patrick, *Saint Patrick: His Confessions and Other Works* (Catholic Book Publishing Corp., 2009), 13.

46. Saint Alphonsus Liguori, *The Way of the Cross* (Charlotte, NC: TAN Publishers, 2009), 15.

47. A. W. Tozer, *The Pursuit of God.*

48. Psalm 34:11 (NKJV) says, *"Come, you children, listen to me."* David also made this connection of children coming to God. It is instinctive for a child to come to his father. When we lose this instinctive "looking unto the Father," we know we have lost the childlike disposition that discovers God.

49. Saint Bernard of Clairvaux, *Sermons on the Song of Songs* (Collegeville, MN: Liturgical Press, 1971).

50. Only His kiss can cure you. Only His kiss can kill you and raise you again into Him.

51. Myrrh is a burial spice, also speaking of Christ's burial and suffering. His kiss, dripping with myrrh, is the secret to joyful perseverance in trials and tribulations in this life, and it is the only thing that keeps the old man dead. If we are not kissed, we will always see the old man over our shoulder.

52. His wounds are the revolving door where I can enter into His heart and make my home in Him. His bleeding wounds invite me into the ecstasy of His presence, where I can abide forever with Christ, the Rock of habitation, my safety, my surety.

53. Jeanne Guyton, *Madam Guyton, A Short and Easy Method of Prayer;* https://ccel.org/ccel/guyon/prayer/prayer.iii.html; accessed March 2, 2024.

54. *"Henceforth there is laid up for me the crown of righteousness, which the Lord, the righteous judge, will award to me on that day, and not only to me but also to all who have loved his appearing"* (2 Timothy 4:8 NKJV). This speaks of loving the appearances of Christ while living, not just at the final judgment.

55. Andrew Bonar, *Memoir and Remains of R. M. M'Cheyne* (Carlisle, PA: Banner of Truth, 1966); https://www.monergism .com/memoir-and-remains-rev-robert-murray-mcheyne; accessed March 2, 2024.

56. In the original language, the Ephesians are not mentioned in what we know as the book of Ephesians. What we do know is that it was carried to the region of Colossae by Philemon. Some theologians believe that the book of Ephesians was actually delivered to the Laodiceans.

57. They would have known the standard, because in Paul's letter to them He described the gift of apostles in Ephesians 4:11 as a gift from God.

58. Ruth Paxson, missionary, Bible teacher, author.

59. Adam Hadhazy, "Why Does the Sound of Water Help You Sleep?" Life's Little Mysteries: LiveScience.com, January 18, 2016; https://www.livescience.com/53403-why-sound-of -water-helps-you-sleep.html; accessed April 8, 2024.

60. Told by Dr. Michael L. Brown during school at Brownsville Revival School of Ministry.

61. This is called the Law of First Mention. It is premised on the idea that when a subject is mentioned for the first time in Scripture, it becomes the key to interpreting all the future mentions.

62. Helen Howarth Lemmel, "Turn Your Eyes upon Jesus," 1922.

About Eric Gilmour

Eric Gilmour is an author, musician, and itinerant speaker who travels domestically and internationally. He and his wife, Brooke, are the founders of Sonship International, a teaching ministry committed to strengthening the Church. Their hearts are to bring the Church into a deeper experience of God's presence in their daily lives. With more than 100,000 subscribers on YouTube, Eric's music and teachings have aided millions of people in resting in the presence of God.

Eric, Brooke, and their two daughters, Madison and Lia, reside in Orlando, Florida. They have two golden retrievers, Mia and Oakley. When he's home you can find him spending time with his family, reading, and/or with a camera in his hand filming or taking pictures, namely in the golden hour.

About Eric Gilmour

YOUR
Prophetic
COMMUNITY

Sign up for a **FREE** subscription to the Destiny Image digital magazine and get awesome content delivered directly to your inbox!

destinyimage.com/signup

Sign up for Cutting-Edge Messages that Supernaturally Empower You

• Gain valuable insights and guidance based on biblical principles
• Deepen your faith and understanding of God's plan for your life
• Receive regular updates and prophetic messages
• Connect with a community of believers who share your values and beliefs

Experience Fresh Video Content that Reveals Your Prophetic Inheritance

• Receive prophetic messages and insights
• Connect with a powerful tool for spiritual growth and development
• Stay connected and inspired on your faith journey

Listen to Powerful Podcasts that Propel You into God's Presence Every Day

• Deepen your understanding of God's prophetic assignment
• Experience God's revival power throughout your day
• Learn how to grow spiritually in your walk with God

In the Right Hands, This Book Will Change Lives!

Most of the people who need this message will not be looking for this book. To change their lives, you need to **put a copy of this book in their hands.**

Our ministry is constantly seeking methods to find the people who need this anointed message to change their lives. **Will you help us reach these people?**

Extend this ministry by sowing three, five, ten, or *even more* books today and change people's lives for the better! Your generosity will be part of catalyzing the Great Awakening that many have been prophesying and praying for.

From
Corey Russell

Unlock Realms of Glory through Praying in Tongues!

Is your vision of praying in tongues too small? Is it unbiblical?

Too often we, as believers, avoid praying in tongues due to confusion or misunderstanding. Yet we've unknowingly laid aside one of the most powerful tools in our spiritual arsenal. This gift brings us out of the flesh and into the Spirit—enabling us to pray from a position of victory, rout the spiritual forces of darkness, and experience a richer relationship with the Lord.

In *Praying with the Holy Spirit,* Corey Russell, a key intercessor and leader, shows you how to activate this supernatural gift, opening up new depths of intimacy with God and igniting you to pray with unshakable fervency, authority, and confidence against any enemy scheme.

Based on his bestselling book *The Glory Within*, this 40-day guided devotional journal takes you on a life-changing journey into the heart of what it means to pray in tongues—and how to do it effectively.

Don't settle for a powerless prayer life. It's time to engage the Spirit, unlock new realms of glory, and unleash the supernatural power of praying in tongues in your world.

Purchase your copy wherever books are sold